CW00971959

GREAT WESTERN LOCOMOTIVES
ON THE MAIN LINE

SCENES FROM AN EDWARDIAN RAILWAY

PETER DARKE

Ian Allan
PUBLISHING

Contents

First published 2012

ISBN 978 0 7110 3538 6

© Peter Darke 2012

Published by Ian Allan Publishing

an imprint of Ian Allan Publishing Ltd, Hersham, Surrey, KT12 4RG

Printed in England by Ian Allan Printing Ltd, Hersham, Surrey, KT12 4RG

Distributed in the United States of America and Canada by BookMasters Distribution Services

Visit the Ian Allan Publishing website at
www.ianallanpublishing.com

COVER IMAGES:
FRONT See page 54.
BACK ABOVE See page 42.
BACK BELOW See page 59.

MIX
Paper from
responsible sources
FSC® C014615
www.fsc.org

Foreword

A. N. M. (ARTHUR) GARRY was born in 1890 and raised near Reading, close to the GWR main line out of Paddington. His grandfather was Rector of the parish of Taplow in the Edwardian period, during which Arthur won a scholarship to Eton College, from Summer Fields School in Oxford.

From Eton Arthur won a scholarship to King's College Cambridge, whence he was in colonial service, and worked in North Borneo for at least 20 years, finally as a member of the legislative council there. In 1921 he married a doctor's daughter from Minehead, Somerset, and retired there before World War 2. He died in 1969, and his widow passed some of his photographic albums to my father, to be passed on to me later. I do not know how he became a railway enthusiast, but it is possible that his grandfather was also a GWR fan.

Arthur Garry – on the occasion of the Summer Fields School (Oxford) centenary celebrations in 1964, when he was 74 years old.

I made Arthur's acquaintance when I was a teenage 'trainspotter' living in Minehead in the 1950s. He became aware that I was a GWR enthusiast, and he started to share some of his wide knowledge of the railway with me, including an introduction to the delights of summer Saturday traffic at Taunton. We always travelled to Taunton, naturally, by what is now the West Somerset Railway. He was a very early member of the Railway Correspondence & Travel Society, formed in 1925, and frequently travelled the length and breadth of the UK on their excursions, often along obscure country lines that would soon be closed, in the 1950s.

Arthur was acquainted with some notable early railway enthusiasts, including Tom Rolt and H. M. Le Fleming. However, when I went up to Bristol University in 1961 to study veterinary medicine I lost touch with him. I would welcome any more information about this helpful and knowledgeable gentleman, and feel very privileged that some of his photographic albums were bequeathed to me. I am also sure that he would have been pleased to have learned that his photographs have found a wider audience, and I count myself lucky to be able to do this.

I was delighted to be invited by Ian Allan to publish some of his pictures. While the standard and quality of the photography may sometimes be disappointing, I suspect that Arthur took his photographs more for personal satisfaction and memory than with a view to publication. Furthermore, the limitations of amateur photography a century ago, with what appears to have been a typical plate camera, must be accepted. The shutter speed on this camera would have been very slow, as any shots of moving trains show movement of the subject, even on sunny days.

It is noticeable that, in his brief album captions, Arthur used terms such as 'Bogie Single' (rather than '4-2-2') and 'coupled in front with trailing bogie tank' for an 0-4-4T, as the Whyte notation for describing locomotive wheel arrangements was not published until later. No specific dates appear, but the albums were each dated, the most productive years for steam shots being 1906 and 1907.

Most of the pictures reproduced in this book are of stationary subjects and are mainly portraits of locomotives, taken from the classical front three-quarter view, rather than of complete trains. This can be disappointing to those of us interested in period shots that might show details of the carriages or wagons making up a train, but it is inevitable, given the limitations of the slow shutter speed. It also seems that Arthur focused deliberately on locomotives that were close to withdrawal. Furthermore, it was not just the large express engines that interested him but also the humble shunting tanks, and this is helpful to us. The Edwardian period on the GWR was fascinating in many ways, and not a little exciting.

Arthur's albums contain mostly photographs obviously taken by him, but I have also found a number of better-defined portraits of locomotives that appear to have been posed. I suspect these may have been acquired as commercial postcards. I have no intention of breaching copyright, which is generally held to have lapsed 70 years after the death of the photographer, but it is quite possible that some of these pictures have been published previously, and if anyone is concerned at what may appear to be plagiarism, I can only apologise. I hope that they can accept that these contribute to this survey of Edwardian traction for the benefit of all.

The photographs in Arthur's later volumes, dating from the 1960s, show ex-GWR locomotives laid up in sidings all over the former GWR territory. How many classes Arthur must have witnessed in their last throes, and how sad it must have been to see locomotives that he had first seen as brand-new now awaiting their fate!

For me it is thus a great pleasure to share the delights of the GWR as seen through the eyes of a young enthusiast, 50 years before I experienced similar pleasures. As a tribute to the friendship and advice received from Arthur Garry when I was young, I am delighted to dedicate this book to him. Additionally, in line with what I anticipate might have been Arthur's wishes, I intend to contribute my fee for this book to the West Somerset Steam Railway Trust (*www.wssrt.co.uk*) at Williton.

Peter Darke

BICKNOLLER, SOMERSET

OCTOBER 2011

Acknowledgements

I appreciate very much the help that I have received in assembling and commenting on the photographs that appear in this book. First, I wish to thank Mr Peter Waller of Ian Allan Publishing Ltd for encouraging me to undertake the publishing of Mr Garry's photographs. In particular, Laurence Waters, a fellow-member of the Great Western Society, has helped me to interpret the location of some of Mr Garry's photographs, as has Stephen Cooper over locomotive allocations in the Edwardian period. I am also very grateful to a former school colleague, Neil Wooler, who originally introduced me to the many mysteries of steam traction in the 1950s; much more recently he helped me by reading my draft manuscript, and suggesting useful amendments and improvements. David Randles kindly offered me access to some of his extensive railway literature, which helped me frequently in my interpretation of some of the locomotives and rolling stock in Mr Garry's photographs. And I am grateful to my sister Charlotte Peters who helped to advise me on book layout and cover design. Finally, I wish to thank my wife Carole for her co-operation and endless patience in tolerating my passion for all things Great Western.

Bibliography

Clark, R. H.: *An Historical Survey of Selected Great Western Stations* (four volumes) (Oxford Publishing Co, series commencing 1976)

Haresnape, B., and Swain, A.: *Churchward Locomotives* (Ian Allan, 1976)

Holcroft, H.: *An Outline of Great Western Locomotive Practice, 1837–1947* (Locomotive Publishing Co, 1957)

Nock O. S.: *Standard-Gauge Great Western 4-4-0s* (two volumes) (David & Charles, 1977)

Russell, J. H.: *A Pictorial Record of Great Western Engines* (two volumes) (Oxford Publishing Co, 1986)

Vaughan, A.: *A Pictorial Record of Great Western Architecture* (Oxford Publishing Co, 1977)

Whitehouse, P., and Thomas, D. St John: *The Great Western Railway – 150 Glorious Years* (David & Charles, 1984)

Anon: *Locomotives of the Great Western Railway* (Railway Correspondence & Travel Society)

Part 1: Preliminary Survey (1951)
Part 4: Six-wheeled Tender Engines (1956)
Part 5: Six-coupled Tank Engines (1958)
Part 6: Four-coupled Tank Engines (1959)
Part 7: Dean's Larger Tender Engines (1954)
Part 8: Modern Passenger Classes (1953)
Part 9: Standard Two-cylinder Classes (1962)
Part 12: A Chronological and Statistical Survey (1974)

Introduction

The Great Western Railway (GWR) was founded in 1833 by a group of businessmen to link Bristol with London by the then new mode of transport, the railway. Its Act of Parliament was granted in 1835 and Isambard Kingdom Brunel was employed as Engineer. He laid out what was to be one of the first high-speed lines in the world, choosing a route with generally straight alignment and few major gradients.

Bristol, the largest commercial town in the west of England, had a well-established and sheltered port. The GWR Board anticipated regular transatlantic passenger trade between Bristol and the United States, which would be enhanced by a high-speed rail connection with the capital.

Brunel was ambitious and unconventional, choosing the broad track gauge of 7ft 0¼in rather than the more normal and later-to-be-standardised gauge of 4ft 8½in. Initially this provided the stability that Brunel was seeking for high-speed trains, and the GWR was providing express passenger services running at an average speed of 50mph as early as the 1840s. However, the inconvenience of a railway that could not be connected with the rest of the national system emerged increasingly, as the network expanded. The GWR started to compromise by laying a third rail to the track to accommodate standard-gauge trains which ran through to the lines of other companies. This was a mixed-gauge solution that could be tolerated for a while, but the company came under increasing pressure and finally converted fully to 4ft 8½in gauge, which had by then become the conventional standard, yielding completely in 1892.

Traffic was growing steadily, and the company had a good name for customer service in the rural West Country districts that it mainly served. It was not heavily challenged by competition in that area, after it had seen off or absorbed adversarial challenges in mid-century.

Developments at the end of the 19th century

In the late Victorian period a certain amount of conservatism was expressed not only in the carriages, but also in the locomotive designs, in which the GWR had been somewhat pre-eminent in the days of Daniel Gooch's reign as Locomotive Engineer on the broad gauge. This had followed the rather unsuccessful early period of Brunel's locomotive specifications.

By the late Victorian era William Dean was in charge of locomotive development. He was capable of producing functional locomotives of some beauty in this era of the single-driver locomotives (typically 2-2-2s, and later 4-2-2s) for passenger work. However, by the turn of the century the GWR was following trends, rather than setting them, in developing four-coupled locomotives for extensive use. These 2-4-0s, and more significantly, 4-4-0s, were the general rule for passenger traction on most of Britain's railways by the early 20th century. The decline in use of Singles and the rise of four-coupled and then six-coupled tender engines through the turn of the century into the Edwardian period is charted in Table 6 in the Appendices.

The rest of the traffic was handled by numerous 0-6-0s, many of which were double-framed, mainly built to George Armstrong's design at Wolverhampton Works, and many tank engines, principally 2-4-0 side tanks from Swindon as well as 0-4-2 side tanks from Wolverhampton. These worked routine local passenger services while plentiful and varied types of 0-6-0 saddle tanks were employed on lighter work and shunting. Most of the latter were rebuilt as, or replaced by, pannier tanks.

A characteristic of the GWR was to 'convert' some broad-gauge locomotives to standard gauge. Some of these had been designed and built so as to be re-gaugeable, and 20 of the Armstrong 'Standard Goods' were converted from standard to broad gauge in the 1880s only to be converted back to standard gauge! Some 0-4-2 tanks were converted to standard-gauge 2-4-0 and 4-4-0 tender locomotives.

Bogie suspension became the norm for main-line carriages, providing a far smoother and safer ride than the carriages previously equipped with a mere four or six wheels, with crude suspension. These older carriages were generally relegated to branch line trains, or secondary, stopping, main-line services, early in the 20th century.

The arrival of the Edwardian period early in the 20th century can arguably be considered a 'golden era' in the UK. Certainly, it was for those families that were adequately wealthy, buoyed up by excellent trading conditions, for commerce with the Empire had been developed considerably, with the aid of industrialisation, through the Victorian age. The economic strength of the *Belle Epoque* was expressed in design and architecture, and not for nothing was the glorious *art nouveau* a dominating theme. As far as the railways were concerned, the wealthier public also became increasingly keen on adopting the well-developed rail system for travel and trade, internationally as well as nationally. The GWR prospered in this era as in almost no other period after the end of the broad gauge, and 1913 represents the year in which GWR rail traffic appears to have peaked, just prior to the horrors of World War 1 which nearly bankrupted the UK of talent and meaningful commerce.

Main-line route development

Alongside these developments was a very expansive plan of improvements to the alignment and routeing of some of the GWR main lines. Not without good reason did some nickname the GWR the 'Great Way Round', mainly because the route that the GWR was obliged to use to reach the West Country was the original line via Bristol. The extension of this railway to the west was mainly through associated but initially and nominally independent companies, such as the Bristol & Exeter Railway, the South Devon Railway, and the Cornwall Railway. These lines were all built to the broad gauge, and were therefore compatible with the GWR.

From the mid-19th century the GWR was running trains from Paddington right through to Penzance via Bristol, Exeter and Plymouth. However, as through traffic developed during the century, it was challenged by competition from the London & South Western Railway (LSWR), which ran from Waterloo to Plymouth, North Devon and North Cornwall via Salisbury and Exeter, a shorter and therefore potentially faster route, so the GWR management sought to improve their routeing. Similarly, competition for traffic to the ever-more-prosperous and commercially important West Midlands was created by the London & North Western Railway between Euston and Birmingham and Wolverhampton.

The GWR Board's response to these challenges was adventurous: lines were planned to cut across

country so that trains might speed 'as the crow flies'. These expensive and ambitious plans were intended to provide new stretches of well-aligned main line over which expresses might run at competitive speed, and freight trains might be able to run at less cost, owing to the reduced mileage to be covered. Whether the GWR ever recouped its considerable investment in these ambitious new cut-off lines is a matter for debate.

The most notable lines constructed during this era were the extension and upgrading of the 'Berks & Hants' line from Reading via Westbury and Castle Cary to Taunton. This included new track to pass from Patney (where the existing line to Devizes would form a junction) to Westbury, where the main line to Weymouth would be joined, and from Castle Cary to Cogload, near Taunton, which provided a saving of approximately 20 miles between Reading and Taunton, compared with the journey via Bristol. Similarly, when fully opened in 1910, the Chiltern cut-off between Princes Risborough and Aynho (south of Banbury) via Bicester provided connections with the Great Central Railway and saved some 30 miles over the traditional route to Birmingham via Oxford.

Finally, when opened in 1903, the South Wales Direct route between Wootton Bassett and Patchway, north of Bristol, via Badminton, saved approximately 10 miles. This also avoided the slightly tortuous route via Bath and the outskirts of Bristol that provided the traditional approach to the Severn Tunnel via Chippenham and Bath. This route was becoming very congested with South Wales traffic, following the opening of the Severn Tunnel in 1886. Until some of these cut-off lines were completed all traffic out of Paddington had to pass through Slough and Taplow *en route* to the west and the Midlands. Mr Garry will thus have witnessed the passage of a large variety of GW trains.

Another less prestigious line was opened in 1906, between Bearley Junction (north of Stratford upon Avon) and Cheltenham. This was built as a main line to save charges raised by the Midland Railway, whose tracks had previously been used between Birmingham and Bristol, or the expense of using the much longer GWR route via Hereford. When this route, known as the Honeybourne line, opened, services of express and freight trains were developed between the Midlands and South Wales, and the Midlands and the South West of England.

Developments in GWR stations and maintenance facilities

Further expenditure at this time was required for stations on some of the new lines, including enlargements of existing premises. For example, Badminton, Birmingham (Snow Hill), Gerrards Cross, Honeybourne, Newbury, Reading, Ross-on-Wye, Westbury and Windsor, were all built or rebuilt at about this time. Furthermore, contemporary with modern locomotive construction and maintenance, some extensive new locomotive depots were provided at Old Oak Common (for Paddington), Oxley (for Wolverhampton), Aberdare, Tyseley (for Birmingham), and St Philip's Marsh (Bristol). Additional, less ambitious structures were also built at Leamington, Fishguard, Cheltenham, Carmarthen, Severn Tunnel Junction and Banbury, during the Edwardian period.

Late-Victorian GWR locomotive developments (the Dean era)

Behind the development of better maintenance facilities was the Locomotive, Carriage & Wagon Superintendent (LCWS), as the chief mechanical engineer's post was described at the time. In the Edwardian era the LCWS was G. J. Churchward, who had come to Swindon as an assistant from an engineer's post on the South Devon Railway when it was taken over by the GWR in 1877. Churchward was appointed as the works manager at Swindon in 1896, working as chief assistant to the LCWS at the time, William Dean. Dean had been appointed to this post in 1877, but by the end of the century, his health was reputed to be failing.

Dean had continued to build lightweight express engines (2-2-2s, 2-4-0s and 4-2-2s) until 1898. The advantages of single-driver locomotives was that they were considered to be free-running at speed, and that with the small boilers that were used at the time, large driving wheels could be employed, up to 8ft in diameter. In 1904 'Bogie Single' (4-2-2) No 3065 *Duke of Connaught* was reported to have run from Bristol to Paddington at an average speed of 71.3mph, albeit with a lightweight load of 120 tons. It was claimed to have reached a maximum of 91.8mph on this journey, with an 'Ocean Mails Express'. This was part of a run from Plymouth to Paddington (246 miles via Bristol) in 227 minutes, the first part of which involved the record created by 4-4-0 No 3440 *City of Truro*, which covered the 127 miles from Plymouth to Bristol in just over two

hours, averaging more than 60mph and achieving a claimed maximum of 100mph. The Singles were effectively high-geared, and they provided the possibility of high-speed running without particularly high velocities being required of pistons, valves or valve gear, in an era when lubrication and metallurgy had perhaps not kept pace with the demands of higher speed (*see* Chapter 1).

However, by the turn of the century, increases in passenger traffic and refinements in coaching stock required an increase in length and weight of trains, and single-driver locomotives demonstrated limitations in adhesion for starting trains from a standstill, and for hill-climbing. For this reason four-coupled driving wheels were increasingly being adopted for express work, starting with modest 2-4-0s for mixed-traffic work, but soon incorporating a front bogie for better tracking and stability, leading to the construction of numerous 4-4-0s at Swindon from 1895 onwards, for express and mixed-traffic work (*see* Chapter 2, and Appendices Table 6).

These locomotives were mainly of double-framed construction, a hangover from broad-gauge days. Although the 7ft gauge had been forsaken by the GWR as late as 1892, new locomotives had been constructed for this gauge as recently as 1888, albeit as 2-4-0 inside-cylinder 'convertibles' that could later be adapted to the standard gauge. Within another decade, however, six driving wheels would be required for adequate adhesion in express locomotives, as demonstrated by Churchward's excellent, high-performing 'Saint' and 'Star' 4-6-0s (*see* Chapter 3).

The late 19th century had been a productive period at Swindon, with the construction of two main-line locomotive types – large-wheeled 2-2-2s and 4-2-2s – as well as some 2-4-0s, for passenger work, and a steady supply of 0-6-0s for main-line freights (*see* Chapter 4). Construction of large numbers of inside-cylinder double-framed 4-4-0 locomotives started in 1895, just as Churchward took control. Many of these locomotives were still working 50 years later.

A large number of tank engines were also produced during this period. These were mainly 0-6-0 saddle tanks, construction of which began mid-century, ceasing in about 1901, and 'Metro' 2-4-0 and '517' 0-4-2 side tanks, which were built for light passenger services, from 1869 to 1899 (*see* Chapter 6). These remained in use until the middle of the 20th century. Although one or two individual pannier tank engines were built at the turn of the century, general construction of this type did not supersede the use of saddle tanks until after this era.

Wolverhampton Works enjoyed a certain amount of independence from Swindon in the Victorian era. Under the control of George Armstrong, who had been appointed in 1864 to replace Daniel Gooch, the majority of the locomotives constructed there were tank engines and goods 0-6-0s. Some accounts suggest that the tolerances and standards of construction may have been at variance with those adopted at Swindon, perhaps because Wolverhampton was generally responsible mainly for heavy locomotive overhauls rather than new construction. However, following the end of the Armstrong era in 1897 the influence of Wolverhampton on locomotive design declined sharply.

The Edwardian period also saw the widespread introduction of more modern bogie carriages, in the form of the Dean-designed 'Dreadnought', 'Concertina' and 'Toplight' corridor and non-corridor stock, the last 'Clerestory' coaches being constructed by the GWR in 1904.

The Churchward era

Soon after the turn of the century, in 1902, William Dean was replaced as Locomotive Superintendent of the GWR by his assistant, G. J. Churchward. Here was a man in tune with his time, and he appears to have been well supported by a management who recognised the need to finance expansion, and to accommodate and benefit from the increased flow of traffic, both freight and passenger.

With Dean's failing health, Churchward had been able to develop his own ideas of locomotive construction from about 1898. He was not so much an innovator, as a clever evolutionary engineer who used modern principles. Churchward was able to scour the world for the latest ideas in locomotive development, using details from best engineering practice in several other countries, notably the USA and France. He was seeking a combination of efficiency of operation and standardisation of construction. He sought to optimise power output, and minimise both fuel consumption and the cost of maintenance and repairs, with standardisation, so that a minimum of spare parts might need to be stocked. Furthermore, spare parts were constructed to standards and engines assembled to tolerances whereby parts could be fitted in the works

or in depots 'off the shelf', instead of requiring lengthy fitting and 'fettling'.

For Churchward, the appearance and beauty of the locomotives that he designed was of less importance, adopting the principle of 'handsome is as handsome does'. Some of his design practices provoked criticism as they no doubt appeared rather shocking to post-Victorian eyes. For example, the ghastly angular prototype 'Kruger' 4-6-0 freight locomotives (nominally Dean's design), and some of the early 'Badminton' series of passenger 4-4-0s showed little attention to æsthetics. With transition through these double-framed machines Churchward evolved his modern classes of locomotive to standardised designs, which could be manufactured and multiplied on a large scale, but be maintained with standard off-the-shelf spare parts.

Churchward's prototype locomotives

Churchward started developing his plans back in the Dean era, perhaps as a result of encountering difficulties at depots in trying to fit components to locomotives under repair. There was almost certainly a touch of Churchward in the 4-6-0 freight prototype No 36 of 1896, nominally to Dean's design. Churchward then created several more prototypes in 1902/3 (see Table 4), as well as evolving a standard range of boilers to be fitted not only to existing locomotives such as the 4-4-0s but also the prototypes that he was planning. The design of the double-framed 4-4-0s was also refined as nearly 300 were built over a 15-year period, from 1895 to 1910. They received not only modernised boilers but also piston valves in place of slide valves, and, after about 1910, some were equipped with superheaters. These modifications enabled the large-wheeled classes to produce impressive performances on express trains before they were eclipsed from about 1905 by Churchward's new designs.

In line with North American practice, Churchward developed a range of main-line locomotives that used a limited set of standard components. These (with the exception of 4-4-2 No 40) all had two outside cylinders, and only two sizes of cylinder were originally used. These were supplied with steam by modern and efficient long-travel piston valves driven by Stephenson's valve gear located between the frames, driving the outside piston valves through rocking shafts. Churchward also adopted Belpaire fireboxes, which, together with a limited range of tapered boilers, helped to optimise the flow of water through the boiler and to concentrate the water over the hottest part of the fire in the firebox. Furthermore, in his original plans he envisaged only three driving-wheel sizes: 4ft 8in, 5ft 8in and 6ft 8in (give or take half an inch), for heavy (slow) freight work, mixed-traffic use, and express passenger trains respectively, with the axles running in bearings of generous size.

Churchward first developed modern boilers with raised Belpaire fireboxes in the late 19th century for replacement on Dean's engines such as the 4-4-0s and 2-4-0s, starting with a medium-sized boiler for middle-range engines, which was later to become the GWR's Standard No 2. The first application of one of these boilers was to a brand-new and ugly design of 4-6-0, No 36, in 1896, the first example of this wheel arrangement on the GWR, and one of the first in the UK. This type was later more usually used for mixed-traffic or express passenger traffic. Although nominally designed by Dean, it is in contrast to his earlier range of engines, some of which, notably the 4-2-2s, were particularly handsome, and the sharp and severe lines of this locomotive came as a shock to some observers.

Further Churchward developments and adaptation by other railways

Most of these prototypes (see Table 4) were clearly successful. From No 36, No 33 was evolved, and from this was derived the '26xx' ('Aberdare') 2-6-0 goods type. From the prototype express passenger 4-6-0s, Nos 98 and 100 (see Table 4), the impressive '29xx' 'Saint' class was developed. A 'Saint' was later (in 1924) rebuilt with smaller wheels to create Britain's first medium-sized mixed-traffic design, the 'Hall', which was to set a trend throughout Britain. Stanier, a former Swindon man, used this as the basis for his 'Black 5' 4-6-0 on the LMS, which was such a fine class of locomotive that more than 800 were built, and from this was derived the later BR Standard Class 5 ('73xxx') 4-6-0.

From No 99, the prototype 2-6-2 tank, the GWR derived the '31xx' 'Large Prairie' series of mixed-traffic tank engines, and later produced a tender version in the larger-boilered, versatile mixed-traffic '43xx' Mogul. This useful design also impressed Stanier, who produced a similar locomotive for the LMS, the Class 5 Mogul. At Ashford Maunsell and Holcroft (the latter also ex-Swindon), were similarly influenced by the GWR in designing the SECR's 'N'-class 2-6-0.

Finally, from the prototype No 97 2-8-0 evolved the GWR '28xx' class of heavy-freight 2-8-0, from which a clear lineage can be followed through the LMS '8F', WD 2-8-0s and 2-10-0s through to the BR Standard '9F' 2-10-0, all competent, effective and respected machines.

Each of these Churchward classes commanded respect from the men that operated them, for haulage capacity, their reliability and free-running capability, and for economy. Economy was one of the hallmarks of the '40xx' ('Star') four-cylinder 4-6-0s, derived from Churchward's four-cylinder prototype No 40. This was also the forerunner of the 'Castle' 4-6-0 (essentially an enlargement of the 'Star'), introduced in 1923. It was this feature that created interest from the LMS and Southern railways in using the 'Castle' as a basis for new express locomotive designs on their railways in the 1920s.

The 'Star' prototype, No 40, had been built in 1906 as a 4-4-2 for direct comparison with the three French four-cylinder de Glehn compound Atlantics, Nos 102, 103 and 104. These had been imported in 1903 and 1905 to evaluate their reputed ability to run smoothly and economically at speed with heavy loads. However, Churchward found that, with modern, long-travel valves and well-designed steam passages, No 40 and the 'Star' 4-6-0s could operate just as effectively as the French locomotives, without the complications of the compounding that these had employed.

Nonetheless, the French influence on the 'Stars' was very strong, and from the de Glehn Atlantics were derived the principal dimensions and cylinder layout. However, as 4-6-0s the 'Stars' would have demonstrated a better ability than the 4-4-2s to draw trains from standstill and to climb hills, of which there were plenty on some parts of the GWR main lines. Additionally, Churchward may have found that when running over long distances at high speed the four-cylinder 'Stars' required less heavy maintenance than the otherwise similar-sized two-cylinder 'Saints'. Indeed, the 'Stars' were so successful that lineage can be traced on through the GWR's 'Castle' and 'King' 4-6-0s (the latter a more powerful version of the 'Castle') and the LMS 'Princess Royal' and 'Coronation' Pacifics.

Churchward also produced 40 further single-framed 4-4-0s, after the end of construction of the large numbers of this type of double-framed locomotive. This 'County' class was more in line with his standard designs, with standard outside cylinders, boilers, valves and valve gear. These locomotives were required mainly for cross-country services, on lines on which the new large 4-6-0s were not permitted to run. However, the Churchward 'Counties' were found to be unstable at speed, and they were withdrawn after only 20 years in service, being replaced mainly by the 'Hall' class 4-6-0s. Developed from the 'Counties' were the 4-4-2T 'County Tank', also with 6ft 8in wheels, for outer-suburban passenger traffic. In turn, these were replaced by the '61xx' ('Large Prairie') 2-6-2 tank engines. Also built during the Edwardian era were a couple of classes of inside-cylinder tank engine which represent an intermediate stage between the Dean and Churchward locomotives. These were the '3600' class of 2-4-2T, which appeared in 1900-1902, and the '3900' class of Prairie tank, which was a rebuilt form of 'Dean Goods' tender engines (*see* Table 7). The 'Small Prairies' (later the '45xx' class) were introduced from 1906, but, being used on provincial suburban and branch-line work, none appears in Mr Garry's albums.

Preservation of Edwardian locomotives

By the start of the Edwardian era, despite the influx of new locomotives of Churchward design, there was little wholesale destruction of Dean machines, so the variety of traction to be seen on the main line out of Paddington was expanded. Furthermore, until the new 'cut-off' lines were completed, all long-distance trains out of Paddington, even to Birmingham, ran via Reading, so stations such as Taplow must have afforded the opportunity to observe plenty of locomotives, old and new. Although the withdrawal of some of the Victorian types, notably the Singles, started as early as 1904, the majority, including most 2-4-0s, survived until the next decade. A few 7ft Singles were rebuilt as 5ft 2in 0-6-0s.

We are very fortunate that some artefacts remaining from the Edwardian era have been preserved. Although we have lost some of the fine Edwardian buildings, such as Birmingham Snow Hill and Ross-on-Wye

stations, at least a replica of the latter has been re-created at Kidderminster, on the Severn Valley Railway. Of Dean locomotives '2301' ('Dean Goods') 0-6-0 No 2516 is preserved at the STEAM museum in Swindon, while of Churchward locomotives the record-holding 4-4-0 No 3440 (currently No 3717) *City of Truro* is in the National Collection. We are still more privileged in that, at the time of writing, this locomotive is in use on heritage railways, and in 2004, to mark the centenary of its record dash from Plymouth to Bristol, it made some runs on the main line. Furthermore, 4-4-0 No 9017, one of the 'Dukedog' 'Earls' rebuilt from 'Bulldogs' and 'Dukes' in the 1930s, is also in regular use on the Bluebell Railway in Sussex.

One of the earliest Churchward 2-8-0s, No 2807, recently restored to working order from scrapyard condition, is preserved on the Gloucestershire–Warwickshire Railway, while sister locomotive No 2818, part of the the National Collection and on display in the National Railway Museum at York, retains its original, Churchward-era cylinder block, with inside steam pipes. The four-cylinder 4-6-0 No 4003 *Lode Star* is truly one of the stars of the show in the National Collection and is on display at STEAM, Swindon, but sadly will probably never return to steam. However, good progress is being made in re-creating a replica 'Saint', No 2999 *Lady of Legend*, at the Great Western Society depot at Didcot, through conversion of a 'Hall', by fitting larger driving wheels and appropriate equipment.

Regrettably, no original GWR Single is preserved, but a non-working replica of the glorious No 3041 *The Queen* was constructed at Swindon in 1983 for display at the Madame Tussaud's 'Royalty and Railways' exhibition at Windsor & Eton Central station. The locomotive survives as a feature within the restaurant of the Windsor Royal shopping mall, which took over the site in the 1990s, but, regrettably, the tender was scrapped, being considered 'superfluous'.

1 *The Singles*

The Single had a surprisingly long innings, the type being the definitive express locomotive of the Victorian era and used by all the major British railways. The advantage of a single driving axle was that it could be fitted with large driving wheels (typically of 7ft to 8ft diameter), which would minimise piston and valve-gear speed while permitting relatively high train speeds to be attained. Furthermore, large driving wheels could be used within the limitations of the loading-gauge without compromising boiler diameter, at a time when only small boilers were needed. Finally, Singles were notably free-running, making them ideal for express work. Some of these GW locomotives evolved or had been converted from broad-gauge machines.

Towards the end of the Victorian era, passenger traffic was growing fast, requiring more coaches to be hauled, and the ability of these small locomotives to retain adhesion in pulling away from a stop, or in climbing hills, became very limited. None of the GW Singles was capable of generating more than 15,000lb of tractive effort. Furthermore, with the commonly used 2-2-2 wheel arrangement, there was a tendency towards instability at speed, through a rocking motion. Presumably this was accentuated if bearings and motion were worn, and a

locomotive was due for a heavy overhaul. To counteract instability, a bogie was added, to form a 4-2-2 in several classes, and this rebuilding was employed extensively by the GWR, often with the installation of a new boiler.

Limitations of adhesion, and improved engineering in the motion and valve gear both encouraged the adoption of four driving wheels ('four-coupled' in the language of the time), following an American lead. This improved the adhesive qualities and permitted the development of greater power to cope with the longer trains. By the Edwardian era, as new locomotives were built, the numerous Singles were relegated to secondary (semi-fast) passenger trains. The demise of Singles is apparent from Tables 1 and 6.

These small express locomotives were often considered to be amongst the most handsome of engines, but they were built with little or no protection from the elements for the crew. However, by the Edwardian era portrayed here, they had been equipped with some form of cab, albeit somewhat rudimentary!

Several varieties of Single were still being operated by the GWR in the Edwardian period, the most numerous being the 'Sir Daniel', '3001' and 'Achilles' classes. These were withdrawn from service before World War 1.

'69' 2-2-2

No 70 was built in 1855 by Beyer, Peacock & Co to Gooch's specification, as a standard-gauge 6ft 8in Single and was reconstructed in 1895 as a 'River' 2-4-0, *River Dart*. It was involved in a crash at Thingley Junction in 1907, as a result of which it was withdrawn and scrapped. This is probably a commercial photograph, taken before its final rebuild in 1895. Photographs of these locomotives in rebuilt condition appear in Chapter 2.

'378' ('Sir Daniel') 2-2-2

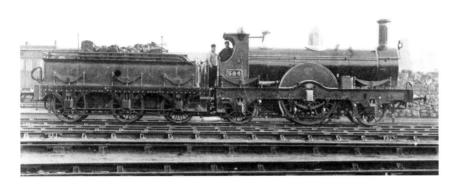

The 7ft Singles of the 'Sir Daniel' class were introduced from 1866. This apparently official portrait of No 584, built in 1869, was recorded before 1901, when this locomotive (in common with most of the class) was rebuilt as an 0-6-0 with 5ft 2in driving wheels. By now the open splashers, which showed the wheel spokes, have been filled in (a case of Victorian modesty?); the Swindon-type boiler was fitted in 1896. The locomotive would finally be withdrawn in 1911.

No 478, built in 1869, recorded at Taunton around the turn of the century, possibly on the occasion of Arthur Garry's first visit to Minehead. This particular 7ft Single was not rebuilt as an 0-6-0 goods locomotive, unlike most of its classmates, and was withdrawn in 1903.

'Queen' 2-2-2

The 'Queen' 2-2-2 design was essentially an enlargement of the earlier 'Sir Daniel'. Featured in this commercial photograph, believed to have been taken at Westbourne Park, is No 999 *Sir Alexander*. Built in 1875, it had been re-boilered in 1900 with this boiler but would be withdrawn in 1904, after covering more than a million miles.

No 1124 passes Taplow at speed on the up main line with an express for Paddington c1906. By now probably allocated to Oxford, this 1875-built 7ft Single had been re-boilered in September 1905. Withdrawal would come in 1912.

Seen on the up relief line at Taplow in 1905 is No 1129, with attentive crew. Built in 1875, the locomotive had been named *Princess May* for a few years in the 1890s and received this Belpaire-type boiler in 1901. It would be withdrawn in 1906.

Another view on the up relief line at Taplow. Like No 1129, No 1130 was built in 1875 and received a Belpaire-type boiler in 1901. Understood to have been allocated to Oxford, for secondary passenger traffic, when photographed in 1906, it was destined to be withdrawn the following year.

'157' ('Cobham') 2-2-2

Similar to the 'Queens', these handsome 7ft Singles, also known as 'Sharpies', were 1879 renewals of locomotives built by Sharp, Stewart & Co in 1862. This photograph of No 158 was taken before the locomotive's first re-boilering, in 1886, and before the wheel spokes were hidden by splashers. Withdrawal came in 1905.

The early standard-gauge 7ft Singles did not survive for long after the arrival of large numbers of 4-4-0s, but No 160, built in 1879, had received a Belpaire-type boiler in 1900 and a reasonably modern cab, as well as enclosed splashers, by the time it was photographed at Evesham. Like No 158, it would be withdrawn in 1905.

No 163 receives attention on the up relief line at Taplow shortly before withdrawal in 1906. Nominally an 1879 'renewal' of a locomotive built by Sharp, Stewart & Co in 1862, it received this Belpaire-type boiler in 1900, losing its dome in the process.

'3001' 2-2-2 and 4-2-2

No 3018 *Racer*, a 7ft 8in Single built in 1892, seen in original form as a 2-2-2 in a commercial photograph taken prior to its rebuilding as a 4-2-2 in 1894. It seems unlikely that such a name would be used in today's Health & Safety-obsessed era. The locomotive was condemned in 1913.

What is believed to be another commercial picture shows No 3017 *Nelson*, later renamed *Prometheus*, in original form as a 2-2-2. Built in 1892, it would be withdrawn in 1908 after a subsequent life as a 4-2-2, no doubt rendered surplus by the influx of 4-4-0s.

A later view of No 3017, recorded after the locomotive's rebuilding as a 4-2-2 in 1894.

No 3013 *Great Britain*, another 7ft 8in Single of 1892 vintage that was rebuilt as a 4-2-2 in 1894. It was taken out of traffic in 1914. This photograph, however, was taken no later than 1906, when the locomotive was re-boilered, losing its dome.

An official photograph of No 3015 *Kennet* of 1892, as rebuilt as a 4-2-2 in 1894 but before being re-boilered in 1902.

No 3015 at Slough in 1905, hauling what is probably a semi-fast train. This locomotive had received its Belpaire-type boiler in 1902 and would be withdrawn in 1908.

No 3026 *Tornado* in rebuilt form, seen on a Bristol express near Acton c1906. Built as a broad-gauge convertible 2-2-2 in 1891, it was re-gauged to standard in 1892, then rebuilt as a 4-2-2 in 1894, as this class had proved unstable at speed. Withdrawal came in 1909.

ABOVE A classic portrait of the handsome 7ft 8in Single. Built as a 2-2-2 in 1892, No 3009 *Flying Dutchman* became a 4-2-2 in 1894, surviving as such until 1914.

No 3002 *Atalanta* at Paddington c1907. Built in 1892 as a 2-2-2 and rebuilt as a 4-2-2 in 1894, it would be withdrawn in 1908.

ABOVE No 3004 *Black Prince* waits with an express train on the down relief line at Slough in 1906, having received this Belpaire-type boiler earlier that year. The carts being transported on wagons in the siding on the left of the picture are of interest. It is a long time since it has been possible to move a farm by rail! No 3004 was built in 1892, being converted to a 4-2-2 two years later, and was withdrawn in 1911.

Built in 1892 and rebuilt as a 4-2-2 in 1894, No 3006 *Courier* was photographed at Paddington in 1907. Withdrawal came in 1914.

'Achilles' 4-2-2

The 'Achilles' class of 4-2-2s, with 7ft 8in driving wheels, was introduced from 1894. The subject of an apparently official photograph taken c1906 at Westbourne Park shed, No 3063 *Duke of York* had been built in 1897 and would be withdrawn in 1912 after a relatively short life.

One of the last of the class to be built, in 1898, No 3074 *Princess Helena* is seen on the down relief line at Slough in 1905. Withdrawal took effect in 1915.

Believed to be at Paddington, No 3070 *Earl of Warwick* had only recently received its Belpaire-type boiler (in September 1905) when photographed. It was in service from 1898 until 1914.

Built in 1894 as *Emlyn*, No 3041 *The Queen* was so renamed for royal duties associated with Queen Victoria's Diamond Jubilee in 1897, when it was posed for this official photograph. Renamed again (upon demotion?) in 1910 as *James Mason*, it was scrapped in 1912, but a convincing static replica (albeit sans tender) can be seen today at the Windsor Royal shopping mall.

No 3052 *Sir Walter Raleigh* was built in 1895 and re-boilered early in 1906, shortly before this photograph was taken near Slough. It lasted until 1913.

No 3054 *Sir Richard Grenville* at Paddington in 1907. Several members of this class were withdrawn after only about 15 years of work, being considered to be too small for 20th-century expresses. This example was in traffic from 1895 until 1911.

Awaiting departure from Paddington with an express train in 1907 is No 3071 *Emlyn*, the name having been transferred from No 3041 (*see page 22*). Built in 1898, it was destined to remain in traffic only until 1914.

The first of this class of Singles to be built as 4-2-2s (as opposed to rebuilt from 2-2-2s), in 1894, was No 3031 *Achilles*, seen in 'shop grey' in this official photograph. Withdrawal came in 1912.

No 3058 *Grierson* at Swindon in 1907, having received this Belpaire-type boiler a few months previously. Built in 1895, it would be withdrawn in 1912.

2 *The four-coupled era*

The limitation of Singles had been clearly demonstrated by the end of the Victorian era, especially when associated with lengthening trains. Most railways looked to develop 4-4-0s and later 4-4-2s (Atlantics) and to a limited extent, 2-4-0s, for express passenger haulage. However, the largest wheels that could be used effectively for four-coupled locomotives were about 7ft in diameter. Like the Singles, these locomotives were generally found to be relatively free-running for express work. Atlantics also permitted the use of a wide firebox over the trailing pair of wheels, which allowed the use of a much less restricted grate, to ensure effective combustion of coal, although, with the exception of *The Great Bear*, this advantage was not adopted by Churchward.

However, during the Edwardian era passenger traffic expanded further, and by the middle of the first decade of the 20th century trains had once again outgrown locomotive capacity, and the ability of four-coupled locomotives to retain adhesion in pulling away from stops, or in climbing hills, was easily challenged. To achieve higher performance and power output, which would require larger cylinders and boilers, together with better adhesion, six-coupled locomotives were developed, initially in the form of 4-6-0s, for express work. There seems to have been considerable concern at the time that the need for heavier valve gear might lead to greater power loss, and that this type of locomotive might prove to be insufficiently free-running to cope with high speeds.

It was at the beginning of this era that Churchward succeeded Dean as Locomotive Superintendent, which explains in part his development of many prototypes. Churchward started by improving boiler design, on what was to be a successful range of 4-4-0s, evolved from Dean's earlier locomotives, using either 6ft 8in driving wheels (for express work) or 5ft 8in (for mixed-traffic work), in such classes as the 'Dukes', 'Bulldogs' and 'Cities' (Table 3). The 4-4-0 was in the ascendancy at the turn of the century, but they were to be rapidly eclipsed on express work by Atlantics and 4-6-0s on the GWR, despite some exceptional performances, such as the famous 90–100mph dash by No 3440 *City of Truro* in 1904. However, 4-4-0s remained in mixed-traffic use until well into the 1950s. By that time, however, *City of Truro* had long since been preserved, and today it remains in working order as part of the National Collection.

Dean also built a number of 2-4-0s, such as the 'River' and '2201' classes of express locomotives and the mixed-traffic 'Stellas' and 'Barnums', at the end of the century (Table 2). These featured frequently amongst Mr Garry's photographs, but the use of this wheel arrangement was already in decline early in the 20th century.

'River' 2-4-0

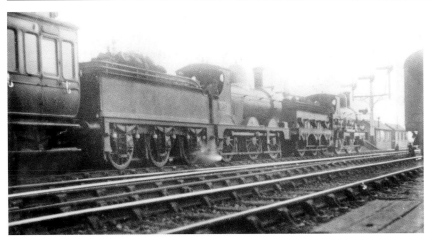

A pair of Dean-era locomotives – 'River' 2-4-0 No 74 and 'Dean Goods' 0-6-0 No 2418 – on passenger duties at Reading in 1907.

The 2-4-0s of the 'River' class, with 6ft 8in driving wheels, were rebuilds of 2-2-2s turned out by Beyer Peacock in the mid-1850s (see caption page 12, Tables 1 and 2). Reconstructed in 1897, No 74 *Stour* was photographed at Reading c1906, by which time the brass dome, formerly polished, had been painted over.

No 74 again, this time on a Southampton-Paddington train on the up main line passing Taplow in 1906. Designed for express passenger work some 50 years previously, these double-framed locomotives maintained some top-link services into the era of the express 4-4-0. *Stour* was condemned in 1918.

Seen on the up relief line at Taplow in 1906 is No 75 *Teign*. As built by Beyer Peacock these locomotives had been 2-2-2s, with 6ft 6in driving wheels; they were rebuilt as 2-4-0s at Wolverhampton Works and were used latterly for secondary passenger services. In the early years of the 20th century this example, built in 1876 and rebuilt in 1895, was allocated successively to Reading and Trowbridge. Re-boilered in 1903, it would survive until 1915.

'806' 2-4-0

ABOVE This photograph, taken at Taplow in 1906, shows Didcot-allocated No 820, an old Armstrong-designed locomotive with 6ft 6in driving wheels and a non-Belpaire firebox. Built in 1873 at Swindon, it had been re-boilered in 1905 and was destined to be withdrawn in 1922, having finally received a Belpaire-type firebox in 1917.

LEFT The '806' 2-4-0s had 6ft 7in driving wheels and were widely distributed in their early years. With the arrival of large numbers of 4-4-0s they were relegated to secondary services. Pictured on the down relief line at Taplow in 1906 is No 808, built in 1873 and destined to be condemned in 1915.

Seeing out its days on secondary duties, Reading-based No 825 of 1873 is seen on a stopping train at Taplow in 1906. It would be withdrawn in the autumn of that year.

'2201' 2-4-0

The '2201' class of 6ft 6in 2-4-0s was almost identical to the '806' class but was attributed to Dean, rather than Armstrong, and was also built at Swindon. No 2212, dating from 1882, is seen shortly before withdrawal in 1904.

ABOVE Reading-allocated No 2206 heads a stopping train on the down relief line at Taplow in 1906. These locomotives were built for express passenger work but were later relegated by the influx of 4-4-0s. This example was in traffic from 1881 until 1921.

LEFT Pictured in wintry conditions at Taplow in 1906, No 2218 had been built in 1882 and re-boilered in 1905. By now based at Reading, it was destined to be withdrawn in 1921, having received a Belpaire-type boiler in 1914.

The '2201s' had 6ft 6in driving wheels and were at home on passenger services, as demonstrated by No 2213 at Reading, where it was based, in 1906. This 1882-built locomotive eventually received a Belpaire boiler in 1914, following which it lasted another seven years.

'717' 2-4-0

Intended for secondary standard-gauge passenger services, the 11 '717s', with 6ft driving wheels, were constructed at Wolverhampton and, unusually, were built with inside frames (albeit double at the front) at a time when most GW locomotives had full-length double frames. This photograph, taken at Oxford c1906, shows Birmingham-allocated No 723. Built in 1872, it would be withdrawn in 1919.

'151' ('Chancellor') 2-4-0

The 'Chancellor' 2-4-0s, eight in number, were built by George England & Co in 1862 as standard-gauge 6ft 6in express locomotives. They had long lives, working mostly in the GWR's Northern section (i.e. north of Birmingham); heavily rebuilt in 1878, this example, No 151, would remain in traffic until 1920. This photograph dates from about 1906.

'3232' 2-4-0

This outer-suburban stopping passenger train, photographed at Taplow, was a typical duty for one of this small class of 6ft 7in passenger locomotives in 1906. Again, the locomotive, No 3236, is spotlessly clean. Completed in 1892 and re-boilered in 1902, it would receive a Belpaire-type boiler in 1916 before ultimately being condemned in 1926.

The '3232' was the last design of 2-4-0s to be built at Swindon and was a development of the '2201', for secondary passenger duties. No 3248 was one of the few examples fitted with Westinghouse brakes in addition to the normal vacuum system. Allocated to Westbourne Park, it would have worked through to other railways, such as the SECR, which used this braking system. Built in 1893, it was withdrawn in 1923. This photograph was taken at Slough in 1906.

'3201' ('Stella') 2-4-0

ABOVE Although the class was built for menial duties (as identified by the lack of brass embellishments), just look at the beautiful finish to the paintwork on 'Stella' No 3503. In common with all others of its type it would later receive a Belpaire-type boiler and superheater. Built in 1885 as a 2-4-0 broad-gauge tank locomotive, it was rebuilt in this form in 1892 and it would be withdrawn in 1929.

BELOW Oxford-allocated No 3515 is seen at Taplow in 1907 with a down stopping passenger train – at the time a typical duty for this 25-strong class of 5ft 2in mixed-traffic locomotives. Built in 1885 as a double-framed 2-4-0 side tank locomotive, it had been rebuilt in 1894 as a 'Stella' and received this boiler in 1905. It was later fitted with a Belpaire-type boiler and superheater and it would remain in traffic until 1930.

As mixed-traffic locomotives with 5ft 2in driving wheels, the 'Stellas' were well suited for duties such as this stopping passenger service, seen at Oxford in 1906. The outside springing, large dome and double frames give these locomotives an ancient appearance, but re-boilering with a Belpaire type in 1909 should have helped. No 3517 had been built in 1885 as a 2-4-0T, rebuilt in 1894 and would be withdrawn in 1919.

The first of the class, built in 1884, No 3201 is pictured at Taplow in mid-1906. It received a replacement boiler later that year and was destined to survive until 1933, the 'Stellas' ultimately being replaced by the 'Bulldog' 4-4-0s.

No 3506 pictured at Slough (where it was based) in 1906 on the up relief line, alongside the Peters factory, where seats for trams and auto-coaches were made. This double-framed locomotive was built in 1885 as a broad-gauge convertible, being re-gauged in 1892. Re-boilered in 1904, it ended its days in 1926.

'Barnum' ('3206') 2-4-0

Pictured c1900, No 3222, one of the 20 'Barnums' built in 1889, received a Belpaire-type boiler in 1901. Here showing a surprising amount of brasswork for a mixed-traffic locomotive, it would almost certainly have lost its shiny dome (and some beading) when re-boilered. Withdrawal came in 1937.

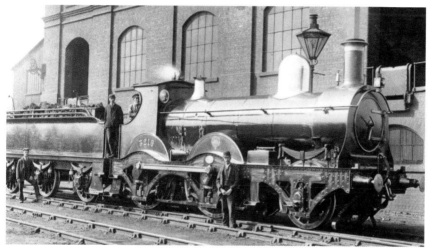

What appears to be an official photograph of one of the later classes with double frames, taken at the end of the 19th century. This is No 3216, which would be withdrawn in 1936, having been fitted with a Belpaire-type boiler in 1907.

No 3207 passes Taplow on the up main line with a stopping train in 1906. Built in 1889, it had received the modern Belpaire-type domeless boiler in 1905. Fitted with 6ft 2in driving wheels, the class worked principally on secondary main-line passenger services, but this locomotive was to end its days on the Cambrian system, in 1933.

Oxford-based 'Barnum' No 3212 heads west from Slough in 1906. This locomotive had received its domeless
Belpaire boiler in 1902, no doubt losing some brasswork in the process, and would be condemned in 1929.

'Armstrong' 4-4-0

Built as one of a class of just four (the others being Nos 7, 8 and 16), No 14 Charles Saunders was one of many
locomotives with a history of rebuilding by the GWR. This official photograph, taken c1906, shows a locomotive
(with a crowded footplate!) that had been constructed as a broad-gauge (convertible) 7ft 1in 2-4-0; in 1894
it reappeared as a standard-gauge 4-4-0; then, in 1917, it was fitted with a taper boiler (with superheater),
new cylinders and 6ft 8in driving wheels to become a 'Flower' express engine, No 4170.

'Duke' 4-4-0

'Duke' 4-4-0 No 3255 *Cornubia* approaches Taplow from the London direction with the afternoon milk empties as, making good use of this four-track main line, '3232' 2-4-0 No 3234 heads a down express in 1906. Both locomotives are immaculately turned out, as was customary at this time.

RIGHT No 3323 *Mendip* at work on the down relief line at Slough in 1906. This 1896-built mixed-traffic locomotive, with 5ft 8in driving wheels, would have its boiler replaced by a Belpaire type in 1907 and later be fitted with a superheater, in this form surviving until in 1936.

BELOW *Mendip* again, this time running light at Reading, where it was based, after re-boilering. Later renumbered 3288, it would be replaced by 'Dukedog' 3200 (9000) in 1936. The work of this class was generally assumed by '43xx' Moguls.

'Bulldog' 4-4-0

An official photograph of one of the 'Bulldog' class of mixed-traffic locomotives, most of which were replaced in the 1930s by Moguls and 'Hall' 4-6-0s. No 3420 *Ernest Palmer*, built in 1903, is here fitted with a Belpaire firebox; it was to receive a tapered boiler in 1910. Later renumbered 3368, it would be withdrawn in 1935.

No 3341 *Mars*, photographed c1906, in early condition with curved frames and a parallel Belpaire boiler, as well as a combined name- and number-plate. Built in 1900, it would be withdrawn as No 3329 in 1932.

No 3427 *Sir Watkin Wynn* at Westbourne Park shed c1906, when three years old. These general-purpose, 5ft 8in-wheeled 4-4-0s, usually with straight frames, had long lives, being replaced mainly by '43xx' Moguls. Built in 1903 and not withdrawn until 1947, this locomotive was latterly numbered 3375.

Weymouth-allocated No 3352 *Camel* heading the afternoon milk empties – typical work for the 'Bulldogs' – on the down relief line at Taplow in 1907. Built in 1899, this locomotive received a taper boiler in 1907 and remain in traffic until 1934.

No 3466 *Barbados* was one of the later 'Bulldogs', delivered in 1904, with a taper boiler. Depicted a couple of years later, it would subsequently be renumbered 3404, in which guise it was destined to survive until 1937. These locomotives were generally replaced by '43xx' Moguls, themselves already being displaced by the arrival of 'Hall' 4-6-0s.

Another early official print in the photographer's collection, dating from around 1905, illustrates No 3339 *Marco Polo*, with combined name- and number-plate. Built in 1900, it received a taper boiler in 1910 and was later renumbered 3327, finally being taken out of traffic in 1936. The later locomotives had straight frames and separate name- and number-plates.

No 3366 *Restormel* rests in the sidings to the east of Taplow while on freight duty *c*1908: no 'hi-vis' required here! Built in 1900, this locomotive, would have a shorter life than did many of the class (some of which were to last into the 1950s), being withdrawn (as No 3354) in 1934 – this despite receiving a taper boiler in 1909 and a superheater in 1911.

'Bulldog' No 3422 *Sir John Llewellyn*, recently rebuilt with a Belpaire-type boiler, and nearly new 'Saint' 4-6-0 No 2917 *Saint Bernard* at Swindon in 1908. The 4-4-0 is on express passenger work, while the 4-6-0 appears to be on pilot duty.

'Badminton' 4-4-0

No 3293 *Barrington* pictured in 1906 in as-built condition, with early-style splashers and parallel Belpaire boiler. Constructed in 1898 and fitted with a taper boiler in 1904, this locomotive would be withdrawn in 1930 as No 4101.

No 3305 *Samson* had been re-boilered with this 'City'-type taper boiler in 1905, dating this photograph to c1906. Fitted with 6ft 8½in driving wheels, the 'Badmintons' (along with the later 'Cities') were used widely on express trains, as denoted by the brass beading on the splasher. Built in 1898, this locomotive would be withdrawn in 1931, by which time it had been renumbered 4113.

No 3295 *Bessborough* at Swindon station in 1907, having had a standard taper boiler fitted late in 1906 to replace its domed parallel Belpaire-type original. Built in 1898, this locomotive would be condemned in 1930 as No 4103.

Although a poor-quality photograph, this is a rare action shot of 'Badminton' No 3301 *Monarch* passing Taplow at speed with an up excursion in 1907. Like her many sisters, this locomotive was employed on fast passenger duties when new in 1898. She had lost her domed boiler in 1902 and would be withdrawn in 1931, having been renumbered 4109 in the interim.

'Atbara' 4-4-0

Like the 'Badmintons', the 6ft 8in 'Atbaras' were used on express workings alongside the 'Cities'. In what appears to be a commercial photograph No 3390 *Terrible* approaches Dunball, near Bridgwater, c1905, in charge of the down 'Cornishman', which in that era ran from Paddington. It is perhaps surprising that the publicity-conscious GWR retained such a name for a front-line locomotive, it actually being named after a Royal Navy cruiser. Built in 1900 and later renumbered 4136, it would be taken out of traffic in 1927.

No 3412 *Singapore* near Taplow in 1906, in charge of the 'South of Ireland Boat Train' to Fishguard Harbour – the type of work for which these locomotives had been built. The train comprises clerestory-roof stock, few GWR trains being furnished with anything more modern at this time. Built in 1901, No 3412 would receive a taper boiler and superheater in 1910, in this form continuing to serve the GWR until 1938. Saddle tanks appear to be shunting nearby.

Another 'Atbara' given the name of a naval cruiser – and one arguably more appropriate for a locomotive – was No 3385 *Powerful*. Built in 1900, it was photographed prior to rebuilding with a taper boiler (in 1905). Note the early-style combined name- and number-plates; also the widespread use of brass fittings, appropriate to a front-line locomotive. However, the 'Atbaras' were soon displaced from top-link work by 4-6-0s, and this example, renumbered 4131, was withdrawn in 1929.

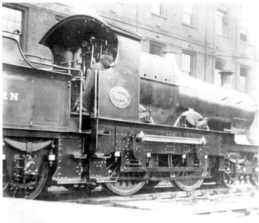

ABOVE An official photograph of No 3380 *Ladysmith* as built, with straight frames and a domeless, parallel Belpaire-type boiler. A taper boiler would be fitted in 1906.

LEFT Built in 1900, No 3380 *Ladysmith* was still on front-line duties when photographed at Paddington, with recently fitted taper boiler, in 1907. Later renumbered 4127, it would be withdrawn in 1929.

BELOW Another bought-in photograph in Mr Garry's collection shows No 3405 *Mauritius* after rebuilding with a 'City'-type taper boiler in1902, when a year old. The brass embellishments were kept well cleaned and polished at this time. Later renumbered 3705, the locomotive would be withdrawn in 1928.

No 3384 *Omdurman* on
duty at Reading in 1907.
Another product of 1900,
it would to gain a taper
boiler in 1910 and a
superheater in 1912
before being renumbered
as 4130. Withdrawal came
in 1930.

Still on front-line duties,
No 3375 *Colonel Edgcumbe*
had recently been rebuilt
with a taper boiler when
captured on film heading
a Birmingham express
near Langley in 1906. This
1900-built locomotive
would be withdrawn
in 1928 as No 4122.

Built in 1900 as an express passenger locomotive, with
6ft 8½in driving wheels, No 3383 *Kekewich* is pictured on
secondary duties on the up relief line at Taplow in 1906.
Fitted with a taper boiler in 1909, this locomotive would
be renumbered 4129 ahead of withdrawal in 1928.

'City' 4-4-0

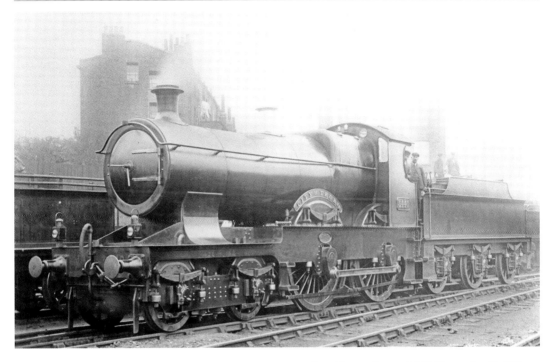

ABOVE One of the most famous of all GWR locomotives, No 3440 *City of Truro* (Swindon Works No 2000) of 1903. This official view, recorded c1906, shows the locomotive before design developments such as the use of superheating and top feed for the boiler, as well as the countersunk rivets. Later renumbered 3717, it was withdrawn in 1931 and retired to York Railway Museum.

LEFT Another 'City' from the 1903 batch, No 3436 *City of Chester,* in an official photograph taken c1906. It was withdrawn in 1929.

No 3434 *City of Birmingham* draws into Paddington c1906 at the head of an express from Bristol. Built in 1903 with a taper boiler, it was destined to remain in traffic until 1930, albeit long since displaced from front-line duties by Atlantics and the 'Saint' and 'Star' 4-6-0s.

A commercial photograph, dating from c1906, featuring No 3437 *City of Gloucester*, built in 1903.

No 3437 *City of Gloucester* again, this time at Paddington station c1908. In common with most of its class it would gain a superheater and top-feed apparatus in 1911. Latterly numbered 3714, it would remain in traffic until 1929. Note the variety of parcels traffic that used to travel by rail!

'County' 4-4-0

No 3474 *County of Berks* photographed c1906 at an unidentified location. Built in 1904, it would be withdrawn in 1930 as No 3831.

No 3473 *County of Middlesex* on the up relief line at Slough in 1907, at which time it was allocated to the London Division. Along with most of its class, this 1904 machine was to gain a superheater and top-feed apparatus in 1911. Subsequently renumbered 3800, it would be condemned in 1931.

In later years the 'Counties' were more commonly employed on cross-country services, but this is another view at Taplow, on the GW main line. Built in 1904 and depicted in 1907, No 3481 *County of Glamorgan* would be withdrawn in 1930 as No 3838.

A recently introduced 'County' was probably not a common sight on a stopping passenger train in the London area in 1906, when No 3815 *County of Hants* was photographed taking the up relief line at Taplow. It would be withdrawn in 1932.

3 *The Atlantics and prototype 4-6-0s*

In view of the successful introduction of Atlantics on other railways, in the USA and on the Continent, as well as the UK, and with their reputation for steady fast-running, Churchward decided to build such a type from his stock of standard parts. Additionally, he wished to use the successful French four-cylinder compound Atlantics as a model against which to test his new designs. These de Glehn-designed machines had a reputation for reliable and economical fast running on long-distance trains in France.

Churchward must have been mightily impressed by the first locomotive, No 102 *La France*, for he later persuaded the GWR board to sanction the importation of two larger engines, Nos 103 *President* and 104 *Alliance*. However, he may already have believed that equal economy could be achieved by simple (non-compound) locomotives with long-travel valves, high-pressure steam and well-designed steam passages. Comparison with the French Atlantics resulted in several of Churchward's early large passenger engines being built as 4-4-2s, with the potential for conversion to 4-6-0s.

Churchward created two main large prototypes with standard components. First came four-cylinder 4-4-2 No 40 *North Star*, later to be rebuilt as the first 'Star' 4-6-0, No 4000, and later still as a 'Castle'. The other was the two-cylinder 4-6-0, No 100 *Dean* (later *William Dean*), which became the prototype for the 'Saint' class 4-6-0s. Several other early members of what became the '29xx' ('Saint') class were also built as 4-4-2s, with the potential to be rebuilt as 4-6-0s. The further development of the four-cylinder 4-6-0s as GW 'Kings' has been well documented, as has the rebuilding of a 'Saint' as the prototype of the numerous 'Hall' class of general-purpose main-line 4-6-0. The 'Star' and 'Saint' classes remained in use until the mid-1950s. No 4003 *Lode Star* has been preserved as part of the National Collection and can nowadays be found in the STEAM museum at Swindon, while a 'new' 'Saint' (No 2999 *Lady of Legend*) is currently being created by the Great Western Society at Didcot, using the frames and boiler of 'Hall' No 4942 *Maindy Hall*.

De Glehn 4-4-2

French-built Atlantic No 104 awaiting departure from Paddington when fairly new, probably during the winter of 1905/6. In their early years these esteemed compounds were allocated mainly to trains to the South West. No 104 was later named *Alliance* and later still carried a typical GWR taper boiler. It was trialled against Churchward's two-cylinder Atlantics.

No 104 passes Slough on an express in 1907. Its career on the GWR spanned the years 1905-28.

Churchward 4-4-2

No 181 *Ivanhoe* in 'workshop grey' for clarity in its official photograph, taken when the locomotive was new in 1905. Rebuilt as a 4-6-0 in 1912 and subsequently renumbered 2981, it would remain in traffic until 1951.

When this scene, believed to be at Slough, was recorded, in the winter of 1905/6, No 185 *Winterstoke* was only a few months old. Built as a 4-4-2, it was converted to a 'Saint' 4-6-0 in 1912 and as No 2985 remained in GWR stock until 1931. Prior to rebuilding, these locomotives were often described as 'Scotts'.

It must have been a rare sight to see a pair of these Atlantics double-heading when almost new in the winter of 1905/6. Here No 185 *Winterstoke* pilots train engine No 190 *Waverley* through Taplow with the 3pm Paddington-Exeter. Allocated to Westbourne Park and Newton Abbot respectively, they were used mainly on the heavy passenger trains to the West via Bristol.

Churchward Atlantics Nos 181 *Ivanhoe* and 190 *Waverley* speed through Slough on the down main in 1907. Like most of the 14 Atlantics (Nos 171/2/9-90) they were rebuilt as 4-6-0s in 1912. Later renumbered 2981 and 2990, they were withdrawn in 1951 and 1939 respectively.

Almost-new No 186 passes Taplow on the up main line early in 1906, before being named *Robin Hood*. The angular shape of the footplating came as quite a shock to some observers at this time, but the turn-out of the locomotive is as immaculate as ever. Converted to a 4-6-0 in May 1912, it was withdrawn in 1932.

ABOVE Running as a 4-4-2 early in 1906, when nearly new, No 182 is seen near Langley at the head of a Paddington-Penzance express consisting of clerestory-roofed stock. Later named *Lalla Rookh*, after an oriental romance by Thomas Moore, this locomotive would be rebuilt as a 4-6-0 in 1912 and withdrawn (as No 2982) in 1934.

BELOW No 40 photographed at Plymouth North Road prior to being named *North Star*, with angular footplating and absence of later boiler modifications. Constructed in 1906 as a 4-4-2, this locomotive was rebuilt in 1909 as the prototype 'Star' 4-6-0, becoming No 4000 in the December 1912 renumbering scheme. Rebuilt again in 1929 as a 'Castle', it would survive until May 1957.

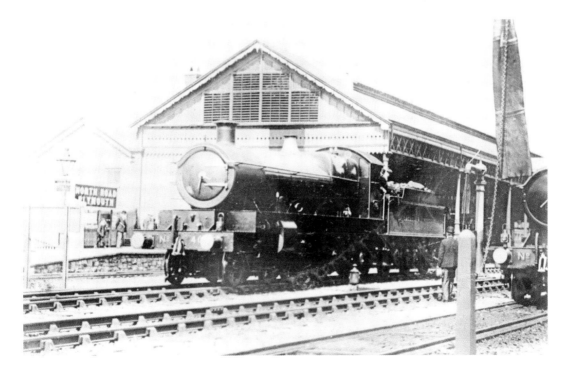

Churchward 4-6-0

ABOVE Churchward's prototype two-cylinder 4-6-0, No 100 *William Dean*, with 6ft 8½in driving wheels (and from which the 'Saint' class was developed), passing Taplow at the head of an express, possibly for Bristol, in 1907. Completed in 1902, it was later renumbered 2900 and was withdrawn in 1932.

BELOW An official portrait of No 175 *Viscount Churchill* in 'shop grey' when newly ex-works in 1905. The angular lines were in stark contrast with the previous express locomotives, especially the Singles. It was not withdrawn until 1944, by which time it was numbered 2975 and named *Lord Palmer*.

No 174 *Lord Barrymore*, built in 1905 as a 4-6-0, seen heading a local train, possibly at Slough, c1906. Later renumbered 2974, it was taken out of service in 1933.

No 2906 when brand-new in 1906, probably at Old Oak Common. Turned out with countersunk rivets, an absence of curves in the footplating or brass beading, in stark contrast with the embellishments on the preceding Victorian passenger locomotives, it also lacks superheating and a top-feed boiler, which has only a short taper. Later named *Lady of Lynn*, it was destined to be one of the last survivors of its class, not being withdrawn until 1952.

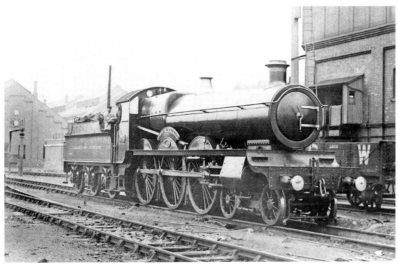

No 2918 *Saint Catherine* in official pose at Old Oak Common shed when new in 1907. The 'Saints' of this batch were built with curved ends to the footplating. This example would be withdrawn as early as 1935.

No 2903 *Lady of Lyons* at the
head of the 'Cornish Riviera
Limited' when new in 1907,
at which time it was allocated to
Plymouth. It would be withdrawn
shortly after nationalisation,
in November 1949.

No 2915 *Saint Bartholomew*
waits to depart Paddington in
1907, shortly after completion
at Swindon. It would remain
in traffic until withdrawn by
BR in 1950.

BELOW Newly built 'Saint'
No 2908 passes Hayes with the
up 'Cornishman' early in 1906,
in the days when this train ran to
Paddington. Named *Lady of Quality*
in October of that year, this
locomotive would remain
in traffic until 1950.

ABOVE No 2908 a year on, at
Reading. The angular lines have
been partially offset by some
brass fittings.

RIGHT Another view of an almost
brand-new 'Saint', No 2911 *Saint
Agatha*, at Swindon in 1907. Fitted
with a superheater and top-feed
apparatus c1912, it would be
condemned in 1935.

ABOVE Double-headed 'Saints' were never a common sight, even during the Edwardian era, so this view of Nos 2906 *Lady of Lynn* and 2923 *Saint George* in charge of a West Country express near Midgham is of particular interest. They were built in 1906 and 1907 and withdrawn in 1952 and 1934 respectively.

LEFT Standing at Paddington c1908, ready to take an express to the West, is No 2927 *Saint Patrick*, then allocated to Cardiff. Note the large stack of empty milk churns awaiting transport back to West Country dairies. Superheated from 1912, No 2927 would remain in traffic until 1951.

RIGHT Recently-delivered No 2914 *Saint Augustine* passes through Midgham station at speed with an express from the West Country in 1907. The train comprises some of the GWR's first non-clerestory stock, which appeared c1905. The locomotive would be withdrawn in 1946.

Seen in its later days, at Taunton, on a stopping passenger service, probably to Bristol, is No 2902 *Lady of the Lake*. By this time, just prior to World War 2, withdrawal of the 'Saints' had begun, but the remaining locomotives had all been all fitted with superheaters and top feed to the boiler. No 2902 would survive until 1949.

A photograph taken at Taunton in 1938 showing 'Star' No 4023 *The Danish Monarch* in its final form, with superheated boiler and top feed but with brass beading removed. This locomotive was originally named *King George* but, along with other members of the class named after kings, was renamed when the '60xx' class was introduced in 1927. It was withdrawn in July 1952.

A portrait of No 4008 *Royal Star* when almost brand-new at its home depot of Old Oak Common c1907.
This particular locomotive was withdrawn in 1935, but 'Star' 4-6-0s continued to work from London to Bristol
and the West until the 1950s.

'Star' No 4003 *Lode Star*
of 1907 heads a stopping
passenger service when
almost brand-new and
allocated to Old Oak
Common. This locomotive
was fortunately not
scrapped when withdrawn
in 1951, instead passing
into the National Collection,
and, following a number
of years on static display
in the National Railway
Museum in York, was
transferred late in 2010
to STEAM, at Swindon.

4 Goods and heavy-freight locomotives

As on other railways, GWR goods engines of the Victorian era were mainly 0-6-0s, whether broad or standard gauge. Double-framed standard-gauge 0-6-0s built at Wolverhampton Works by Armstrong were referred to as the 'Standard Goods', and Dean was responsible for an updated single-framed version at Swindon, the 'Dean Goods'. These lasted until the 1950s, and a representative (No 2516) survives today in preservation at Swindon. The class enjoyed a very good reputation, not least because they were tough and steamed well. However, they were relatively lightweight locomotives, which is partly why they lasted as long as they did, as they were permitted to run on lightly laid track on routes with a 'yellow' restriction, notably in Mid-Wales, for which production of new locomotives would have been too expensive. The 'Standard Goods' were withdrawn much earlier.

Churchward recognised a need for more powerful machines for long-distance freight, and produced two prototypes. First to appear, in 1900, was No 33, a 2-6-0 based partly on an earlier 4-6-0 (No 36), produced by Dean in 1896. It later begat the 'Kruger' and the

'Aberdare' class of Mogul, with two inside cylinders, 4ft 7½in drivng wheels and double frames, related in construction to the contemporary 4-4-0s, but with the smaller driving wheels appropriate to a freight locomotive. Churchward's second prototype, in 1903, was No 97, the outside-cylinder, single-framed 2-8-0, with driving wheels also of 4ft 7½in diameter, from which was derived the standard GWR heavy-freight '28xx' 2-8-0. Considerably more powerful than the 'Aberdares', the locomotives of this class were very successful and economical, being ideal for long-distance main-line work, such as the South Wales–London coal trains, and lasted almost to the end of steam on the Western Region.

In the era covered by this book the 'Standard Goods' and the 'Dean Goods' 0-6-0s were found throughout the GW system on some of the lighter freight and merchandise trains, while the newly built 'Aberdare' 2-6-0s and '28xx' 2-8-0s also appear in some photographs on heavy main-line traffic, including South Wales coal trains. Seven examples of Churchward's '28xx' design survive in preservation, some in working order.

'388' ('Standard Goods') 0-6-0

With its double frames and outside springs, No 433 displays its ancient origins while shunting at Taplow gravel pits c1905, when based at Slough. Some 300 of these 'standard' locomotives with 5ft driving wheels were built at Swindon in the Victorian era to handle the steady growth in standard-gauge goods traffic, on which they were later supplemented by the 'Dean Goods' 0-6-0s. Built in 1868, No 433 would be withdrawn in 1913.

Another of this large class, No 1202 is seen at Taplow on a local passenger working in 1906. As was the case with the later 'Dean Goods', this was a common type of duty for these locomotives. This example was employed by the GWR from 1876 until 1927.

No 39 passing Taplow in 1907, apparently at some speed, with what is described as a 'troop train' (with express headlamps) but which appears to consist entirely of horseboxes – a reminder that in the days before motorised road transport the Army must have run frequent trains to transport its work horses. No 39 had been built in 1876 and would be withdrawn in 1921.

In charge of an up goods, No 696 awaits signal clearance at Taplow in 1907. Built in 1872, it would remain in traffic until 1922.

Possibly acting as station pilot, as indicated by the lamp code, No 670 stands in Oxford station in 1906. This locomotive had been taken into stock in 1871 and would be withdrawn in 1912.

No 500 (with polished dome!) shunting the sidings to the east of the station at Taplow in 1907. The tender is full of good-quality South Wales coal, no longer readily available today. The locomotive had been built in 1870 and would survive until 1921.

Taplow in 1906 – a scene typical of the period. By now allocated to Reading, No 612 had been completed in 1871 and would be withdrawn in 1915.

Built at Swindon in 1872 and fitted in 1902 with a Belpaire-type boiler, No 673 was to serve the GWR until 1924. This photograph was taken c1906, probably near Taplow.

'Standard Goods' 0-6-0 No 495 was built in 1870 and received its Belpaire-type boiler in 1903. Seen in 1906/7 on the main line near Slough with a rake of empty wagons, it was destined to remain in service until 1917.

No 788 passes Taplow on the up relief line with a goods working in 1906. It was in traffic from 1873 until 1908.

'2301' ('Dean Goods') 0-6-0

A typical example of the numerous and popular 'Dean Goods' 0-6-0s, No 2487 is seen at Westbourne Park shed in an official photograph of 1906. Built in 1896, this locomotive would be one of 62 taken over by the ROD (Railway Operating Division), serving in France during World War 1 and again (having been deleted from GWR stock in 1940) in World War 2 as WD No 159, thereafter being exported to China by the United Nations Relief & Rehabilitation Administration (UNRRA).

No 2397, which served the GWR from 1890 until 1938, these 0-6-0s constituting a long-lived and widely used class. This photograph was taken in 1906 at an unidentified location.

No 2455 on a local goods working at Taplow in 1906. Built in 1895, this locomotive would remain in GWR service until 1940, thereafter serving in France as WD No 127 during World War 2 before being repatriated and scrapped.

ABOVE Immaculately turned out, even for a menial task, No 2446 shunts the sidings at Taplow gravel pits in 1906. This 1893 locomotive would be removed from GWR stock in 1940 to serve in France as WD No 178 during World War 2.

BELOW The burnish marks on the tender – unusual for a goods engine – suggest this to be an official photograph of No 2322, taken c1906, shortly after the locomotive received a Belpaire-type boiler. New in 1884, it was to serve in France and then Salonika during World War 1, following which it would return to service in the UK, finally being withdrawn by BR in 1951.

The 'Dean Goods' 0-6-0s were the general workhorses of the GWR. Here No 2473 trundles towards London near Slough with some empty wagons in 1906. Built in 1896, this locomotive had received a Belpaire-type boiler in 1903 and would serve in France during World War 1. Destined to see active service again (as WD No 192) in World War 2 from 1940, it would be repatriated for scrapping following the end of hostilities.

Built in 1892, No 2428 is seen shunting at Taplow c1905. This locomotive was another to see service in France during World War 2, as WD No 155.

No 2465 in Taplow goods yard in 1907, its train including a cattle truck which has been limed as sterilisation after use. Used by the GWR from 1896 until 1940, the locomotive would see active service in France during World War 2 (as WD No 162), subsequently being exported to China by UNRRA.

ABOVE No 2521 heads a London-bound goods train through Taplow in 1907. Destined to be withdrawn by the GWR in 1940, this 1897-built locomotive would serve in France (as WD No 100) during World War 2, later being used in Tunisia and Italy.

BELOW In charge of a goods train, No 2399 heads through Taplow on the down relief line in 1907. The locomotive was most probably allocated to Banbury – a reminder that Midlands traffic still used this route. Completed in 1890, it was to gain a Belpaire-type boiler in 1910 and, following withdrawal from GWR stock in 1940, would be sent to France for service in World War 2 as WD No 94.

'2361' 0-6-0

Although similar in size to the 'Dean Goods' and with 5ft driving wheels, the 0-6-0s of the '2361' class were of an older type of construction, with double frames and prominent outside springs. Mixed-traffic locomotives, they undertook work similar to that of the Dean locomotives; No 2361 is seen in 1907 departing at Paddington for servicing, having arrived with a passenger train or empty coaching stock. Built in 1885, the first of this class of 20 locomotives, it was destined to be withdrawn in 1932.

No 2374 had received its Belpaire-type boiler in 1904. Seen here at Taplow in 1907, it would be withdrawn in 1930.

In charge of a stopping passenger train, No 2375 waits at the signals at Slough in 1906. Built in 1886, it would remain in GWR service until 1938.

Also built in 1886, No 2374 is pictured in charge of an up goods near Slough c1906.

Dean prototype 4-6-0

One of the first 4-6-0s in Britain, built in 1896 as a prototype goods locomotive, with 4ft 6in driving wheels and an experimental type of firebox, No 36 formed the basis of the later 'Kruger' and 'Aberdare' 2-6-0s. Nicknamed 'The Crocodile', it had a short life, working mainly from Swindon on freight trains to/from South Wales, being withdrawn in 1905.

'26xx' ('Aberdare') 2-6-0

Built from 1900 to an otherwise modern design, with contemporary Belpaire-type boiler, the 'Aberdare' 2-6-0s featured somewhat anachronistic double frames and outside springing. As the nickname suggests, these locomotives, with 4ft 7½in driving wheels, were used mainly on South Wales coal trains. Built in 1903 and seen near Taplow in 1905/6, No 2641 was destined to be withdrawn in 1934, though other examples of this class would survive railway nationalisation in 1948.

ABOVE No 2610 was also only a few months old when photographed at Taplow in 1906, heading towards London (where it was based) with a mixed goods. It would be withdrawn in 1935.

LEFT No 2604 shunts the sidings to the east of Taplow station in 1906, when almost brand-new. Possibly because double-framed construction was already dated by the time it was built, it would have a relatively short life for a goods locomotive, of barely 30 years.

No 2649 passing through Slough in 1906 with a goods train typical of the period. Built in 1901 and by now fitted with a new taper boiler, it would gain a superheater in 1911 and remain in service until 1946.

'28xx' 2-8-0

Designed by Churchward, the '28xx' 2-8-0 was a very effective class of heavy-freight locomotive. Here No 2813, built 1905, trundles up the relief line past Taplow towards London in 1907 with a load of coal, most probably from South Wales. These locomotives would give good service to the railways for more than half a century, No 2813 surviving until 1960.

ABOVE Allocated to Old Oak Common, No 2803 passes through Taplow on the up main line at the head of a goods train in 1907. Built in 1905, it would be withdrawn in 1959.

BELOW Also photographed in 1907 when almost brand-new, No 2830 passes through Taplow on the up relief line with a long-distance goods from South Wales. It would remain in traffic until 1959.

ABOVE Bound for London with a long-distance mixed freight, No 2807 passes through Taplow in 1906, at which time it was allocated to the London Division. Built in 1905, it would be withdrawn in 1963, but was destined to survive by virtue of being sent to Dai Woodham's scrapyard at Barry. It has since been restored to full working order on the Gloucestershire-Warwickshire Railway.

RIGHT Captured on camera when just a few months old, No 2827 waits at signals at Reading in 1907. It would be withdrawn by BR in 1958.

5 *Large passenger tank engines*

As commuter traffic developed in the prosperous Edwardian period, so the GWR started to build tank locomotives appropriate for this traffic. This was because the requirement to turn a tender engine at the end of each trip was an inconvenience, and the length of such a locomotive could be a problem at small stations. For a while the existing (Victorian) small passenger tank classes, such as the '517' 0-4-2T and, in the London area, the 'Metropolitan' 2-4-0T ('Metro Tank') managed to cope with the increasing weight of these trains.

Eventually, in 1903, Churchward produced a prototype outside-cylinder 2-6-2T (Prairie tank), No 99, from which were derived the numerous further classes ('31xx' et al) of mixed-traffic tank engine. In 1905, meanwhile, he introduced the similar '22xx' 4-4-2T, a version of his outside-cylinder 'County' 4-4-0. Initially the 'County Tanks' were used almost exclusively on outer-suburban services to/from Paddington, to which they were well suited, having large-diameter (6ft 8½in) driving wheels and being equipped, like main-line passenger tender engines, with water-pickup scoops. However, they may

have suffered the disadvantages that condemned the 'County' 4-4-0 tender engines to an early demise, namely instability at speed and poor adhesion. Furthermore, the Prairies, with their smaller-diameter (5ft 8in) driving wheels, offered better acceleration from the many stops involved in suburban work.

In contrast to the 'County Tanks' the 'Large Prairies', in their various forms, ('31xx', '51xx' and '61xx') lasted until the end of Western Region steam. With their 5ft 8in driving wheels these were regarded as mixed-traffic locomotives and, as apparent from Arthur Garry's photographs, were often to be found on goods work, even when almost new. However, the later '61xx' series (with higher boiler pressure), introduced by Collett in 1931 to take over London-area outer-suburban duties from the aforementioned 'County Tanks', would be confined largely to passenger work.

The 'Small Prairies' ('44xx' and '45xx' classes), introduced by Churchward in 1904 and 1906 respectively, were intended for provincial suburban and branch-line work and were seldom seen in the London area. Three of the original '45xx' design survive in preservation.

'2221' ('County Tank') 4-4-2T

No 2223 was built in 1906 and was captured on film the following year on the up relief line at Taplow. The vent associated with the water-pickup scoop, with which it was initially fitted, can be seen atop the water tank. The locomotive would be withdrawn in 1932.

Developed to handle the outer-suburban semi-fast trains out of Paddington, the 'County Tanks' were withdrawn when replaced on such work by the '61xx' ('Large Prairie') tanks. Pictured at Taplow in 1907, No 2230 worked these services from new (in 1906) until withdrawal in 1932.

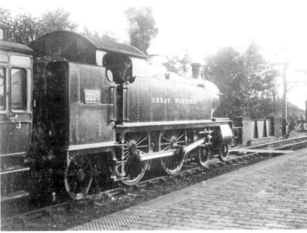

Another example of this specialised, taper-boilered class, No 2226 was photographed at Taplow early in 1907, a few months after it was built. It would be withdrawn in 1934.

Designed for semi-fast outer-suburban workings, the 'County Tanks' had 6ft 8½in driving wheels and, as their name implies, were essentially tank-engine equivalents of the 'County' 4-4-0s. No 2227 was built in 1906, being seen that year seen at Taplow in company with French Atlantic No 103, just visible on the left of the picture. All 30 'County Tanks' would be withdrawn in the early 1930s, this example succumbing in 1931.

No 2230 at Taplow in 1907, when just a few months old. Built in 1906 and allocated to the London Division, it was to serve the GWR until 1932.

'31xx' 2-6-2T

Clearly brand-new, Nos 3147 and 3148 may well have been in the course of delivery from Swindon Works to the London Division when photographed passing through Taplow early in 1906. Later renumbered in the 51xx series, they would be withdrawn in 1953 and 1959 respectively.

No 3143 at Taplow when almost brand-new, in the spring of 1906. The locomotive is devoid of fittings such as front struts and top feed to the boiler (which would be added later) and retains its vertical bunker. Subsequently renumbered 5143, it would be withdrawn in 1951.

LARGE PASSENGER TANK ENGINES

Although later in life used mainly for suburban passenger traffic (the larger-wheeled 'County Tank' 4-4-2Ts being preferred for outer-suburban duties), No 3130 is seen at Taplow in 1907, still devoid of fittings such as front struts, on a goods working. Built in 1905, it would be withdrawn in 1948 as No 5130.

'3150' 2-6-2T

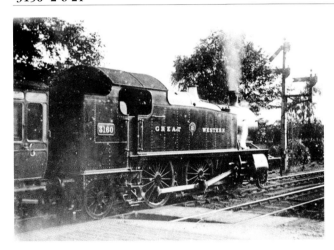

Introduced in 1906 were the 2-6-2Ts of the '3150' class – the first of the 'Large Prairies' that were to become synonymous with GWR suburban trains. Pictured at Taplow when almost brand-new in 1907, having been completed at Swindon earlier that year, No 3160 has already gained certain fittings, such as front struts, that were lacking on the earlier 'Large Prairies' when built. It would be withdrawn in 1953.

Along with the 'County Tanks', some of the '3150s' were among the few tank locomotives to be fitted with water-pickup scoops. Seen at Taplow in 1907 when brand new, No 3166 has been fitted with smokebox front struts – but it still has a straight coal bunker. The top of the water-scoop mechanism is visible above the water tank – this mechanism would be removed a few years later. Discounting five examples rebuilt in 1938/9 (with higher boiler pressure and smaller driving wheels) to form a new '31xx' class, this locomotive would be the first of its sub-type to be withdrawn, in 1947, the majority lasting into BR days.

6 Smaller tank engines

During the Victorian period the GWR built numerous classes of small tank engine. Many of these were 0-6-0 saddle tanks, used primarily for shunting or lightweight passenger or goods work, while others were diminutive 2-4-0 or similar 0-4-2 side tanks, some of which were built with saddle tanks. Attempting to follow the lines of development and the rebuilding of GW tank locomotives can be a frustrating task (*see* Table 6), as, to the uninitiated, most within these two basic types – 0-4-2T/2-40T and 06-0ST – were of very similar appearance.

First, to deal with the lightweight locomotives designed essentially for local stopping or branch passenger trains, the '517' 0-4-2T was designed and built at Wolverhampton Works in the years 1868-85. This class ultimately consisted of over 150 locomotives, of which the initial batches were built as saddle tanks. The later locomotives were built with side tanks, while the earlier locomotives were later rebuilt in this form together with more modern Belpaire firebox boilers. They had driving wheels initially of 5ft diameter – later increased, with deeper tyres, to 5ft 2in. They were also built with no fewer than three different-length driving wheelbases, and some of these also went through a rebuilding process. Most were cabless when built, with just a spectacle plate to protect the driver against the elements. These locomotives were eventually equipped with protective cabs, and many were auto-fitted to operate push-pull trains. A few were also fitted with condensing apparatus to help reduce the exhaust for working through the tunnels of the Metropolitan Railway to Central London stations, such as Aldgate, or goods yards, including Smithfields. From this class were developed the similar '3571' design and, finally, the much-admired – if only for their similarly ancient appearance – Collett '48xx' (later '14xx') 0-4-2Ts of the 1930s, four of which have been preserved (two of them in working order).

The 'Metro' class was visually similar, although it was a 2-4-0T, built at various works including outside contractors, but mainly at Swindon, in the years 1869-99 for similar duties. Most (if not all) of these locomotives were fitted initially with condensing apparatus. They went through similar rebuilding to the '517s', with various sizes of tanks and cabs, and in the Edwardian era were used alongside members of that class, although the majority of those fitted with condensing apparatus were concentrated in the London area.

A large number of small 0-6-0STs, of the '850' and '1901' classes, were introduced by Armstrong in 1874 and built at Wolverhampton Works. These were relatively lightweight passenger locomotives, with 4ft 1in driving wheels (although later rebuilt with 4ft 8in wheels), and many were later auto-fitted for working local push-pull trains. From these designs was derived the '2021' class of 0-6-0ST, most of which were eventually rebuilt as pannier tanks, notably when re-boilered with Belpaire fireboxes.

The other large group of 0-6-0STs – some built as side tanks but also destined to be rebuilt as pannier tanks – were constructed more for shunting and heavier, general-purpose duties. This group (Table 6) was initiated by Armstrong at Wolverhampton Works in 1872 with the '633' and '645' classes, some being built for the broad gauge, but most later converted to standard gauge. They were designed with 4ft 6in (later 4ft 7½in) driving wheels, and from this type was derived the '1813' class, built as side tanks (but later rebuilt with saddle or pannier tanks, and with inside frames) as the '1854' and '2721' classes. These Swindon-built classes were of similar appearance, and all were active in the Edwardian period.

Another type of relatively large 4ft 7½in 0-6-0ST, the 'Buffalo' or '1076' class, was first constructed by contractors for the broad gauge in 1870, but subsequently they were converted to standard gauge. Over 200 were built, the design being based on the previous '1016' class, and from their later form were derived the '1134' and '1813' classes, many of which were auto-fitted. As with other 0-6-0STs, most were converted to pannier tanks, especially when re-boilered with Belpaire fireboxes, and their open cabs were usually later enclosed. A particular characteristic of the '1076' class was that they were double-framed.

Pannier tanks, such a common sight on the GWR in later years, were not part of the GWR scene until about 1911, so do not feature in Mr Garry's pictures from the Edwardian era.

'Metro' 2-4-0T

LEFT A classic view, probably at Slough, of 'Metro Tank' No 1416, built in 1878 and fitted with a condenser c1905. Some 130 of these locomotives were built at Swindon in the period 1869-99. Note the clutter on the front footplating – a spare lamp on its iron, and re-railing jacks, as well as the side-feed for the boiler, the condensing pipework and the toolbox on top of the tank – a far cry from the sleek lines of the Singles! This locomotive would last until 1930.

RIGHT A 'Metro Tank' heading a suburban train on the up relief line at Taplow was a familiar sight in the Edwardian period. Photographed in 1906, No 1415, dating from 1878, has an open cab and is fitted with a condenser for use in the Metropolitan Railway's tunnels – though this will soon be removed.

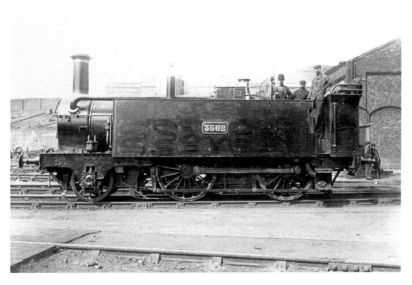

LEFT A portrait of one of the later, Swindon-built suburban 'Metropolitan' or 'Metro Tanks', No 3562 of 1894. Details shown include the condensing pipe and the rudimentary protection for the crew, this latter despite the fact that these locomotives were designed for working through the tunnels on the Metropolitan Railway. 3562 was withdrawn in 1934.

This view of an open-cab condensing 'Metro Tank' in the early 20th century shows the right side of No 967, built at Swindon in 1874 and withdrawn in 1934. Clearly visible is the pattern of the cleaning marks on the tanks and frames, demonstrating a level of attention seldom lavished on tank engines in later years!

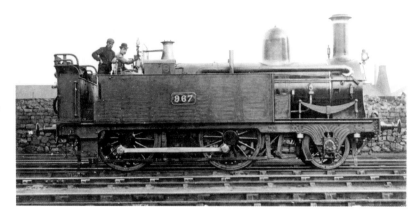

Another open-cab, condenser-fitted 'Metro', No 3581 from 1899, brings a local passenger train into Taplow on the up relief line in 1907. It carries a destination board for Paddington. This locomotive lasted until 1945. Condensers were often removed at this time, after electrification of the Metropolitan Railway.

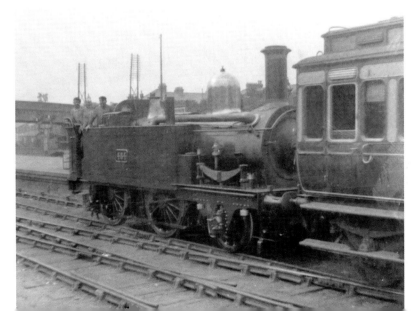

No 464, built in 1869 and withdrawn in 1934, is seen at Slough in 1906, possibly on a Windsor-branch train. The exposure of the crew to the elements is readily apparent, and their experiences in the Metropolitan Railway tunnels on such a locomotive can scarcely be imagined!

On what looks like the embankment in the meadows near Eton College, No 1160 heads the 1.18pm from Windsor towards Slough in 1906. Built in 1882, the locomotive has been fitted with a half-cab.

Its brass dome gleaming, No 972 (built 1874 and withdrawn 1932) waits at Windsor to depart for Slough in 1906.

No 3585, built in 1891, brings yet another suburban train into Taplow station in 1907. Express lamps are carried, suggesting that this was a semi-fast and that the crew will be windswept!

Slough-based No 3564, a condenser-fitted open-cab locomotive built in 1894, seen at its home station in 1906. This locomotive worked until 1944.

Although the 'Metro Tanks' were usually to be seen heading passenger trains, they could also be put to work on shunting duties, as demonstrated at Taplow in 1906 by No 615, built in 1871 and withdrawn in 1931. Cabs were usually fitted when the condensing equipment was removed.

No 1415 on a passenger train at Taplow in 1907, following removal of the condensing apparatus and reallocation to Southall depot. This 1878-built locomotive has by now acquired the ultimate in luxury: a half cab, to limit the crew's exposure to the countryside! 1415 would last until 1938.

'517' 0-4-2T

The '517' 0-4-2Ts might appear to be similar to the 'Metro Tanks', but the wheel arrangement is reversed. Built at Wolverhampton with 5ft driving wheels, and numbering 156 locomotives, they were more closely related to the '48xx' (later '14xx') class which replaced them on lightweight branch trains. No 1466, built in 1883, is seen c1906 at Totnes. It is perhaps worth noting that the subsequent and similar ('48xx') No 1466 is nowadays preserved at Didcot.

No 1472 was an example of one of the Wolverhampton-built lightweight tank engines. Unlike the 'Metros', the '517s' were not equipped with condensers but had more sheltered cabs, as they were usually to be found on rural branch lines rather than in the London suburbs. Built in 1883 and withdrawn in 1934, No 1472 is seen on pilot duty at Reading station in 1907.

Another view of No 1472 shunting at Reading, where the stationmaster is keeping his eye on proceedings.

'1016' 0-6-0ST

The double-framed half-cab saddle
tanks of the Wolverhampton-built
'1016' class were typical of
shunting locomotives at the turn
of the century. No 1045, built in
1870 and withdrawn in 1935, is
pictured at Torquay in 1906 at
the head of the 11am departure
for Newton Abbot. Later versions
were fitted with pannier tanks.
This class would, in the main,
be replaced by '57xx' 0-6-0PTs.

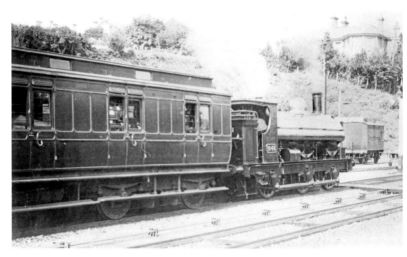

'850' and '1901' 0-6-0ST

The '850' class of lightweight
saddle tanks with 4ft 1½in driving
wheels were constructed at
Wolverhampton Works. No 870,
built in 1875 and withdrawn in
1934, was fitted with a half cab
when pictured at Royal Oak
station in 1906, no doubt on
Paddington station-pilot duty.

No 990, built in 1875 and lasting
until 1931, was photographed
shunting coaching stock at
Paddington in 1907.

Like the '850s', the '1901s' were built at Wolverhampton, the two classes together numbering 170 locomotives. Built in 1882, No 1924 is pictured on pilot duty at Paddington station in 1907, in company with a 0-6-0 tender engine. Like many of these engines, No 1924 would be fitted with pannier tanks in 1912. It ceased working for the GWR in 1938.

'1076' 0-6-0ST

ABOVE Numbering some 266 locomotives built at Swindon, the '1076s' were also half-cab double-framed saddle tanks with 4ft 7½in driving wheels, and some were built as broad-gauge 'convertibles'. Here No 1289, dating from 1878, indulges in some shunting at Taplow in 1906. The tall, copper-capped chimney gives this humble locomotive a somewhat dated look. It would receive pannier tanks in 1925 and last until 1934.

LEFT No 1636 on shunting duty at Twyford in 1907. Shunters would seldom be turned out in such a clean state in later years! This locomotive exchanged saddle tanks for panniers in 1926 and lasted until 1954.

'2021' 0-6-0ST

The '2021' class of lightweight saddle tanks, a development of the '850' class with 4ft 4½in drivers, numbered some 140 locomotives, constructed at Wolverhampton in the period 1897-1905. Built in 1900, No 2083 was recorded shunting at Taplow c1906. Its saddle tanks were replaced with panniers in 1925 and this locomotive would survive until 1951. Many cabs were later enclosed.

No 2081 in original (1900) form, with saddle tanks and half-cab, shunting the sidings to the east of Taplow in 1906. It received pannier tanks in 1926 and lasted until 1954.

No 2132 at work at Taplow in 1907. Built in 1903, it would be rebuilt as a pannier tank in 1922, thereafter remaining in service until 1950, when these locomotives were replaced by new 0-6-0PTs of the '16xx' class.

'1661' 0-6-0ST

The '1661' class of double-framed, 5ft-wheel half-cab saddle tanks was built at Swindon more for general freight duties than pure shunting. No 1681, dating from 1886, is pictured ready for action at Reading in 1906. It received pannier tanks in 1916 and lasted until 1927. These locomotives would be replaced in due course by 0-6-0PTs, notably of the '54xx' class.

No 1680, built in 1886, has a 'shunting' lamp on the spare lamp iron. Note also the well-polished dome – an embellishment that was seldom to be found in later years on such humble locomotives – although the crew might be given a dressing-down for leaving the water-filler open! 1680 received pannier tanks in 1921 and was withdrawn in 1926.

'1813' 0-6-0ST

The inside-framed '1813s' were built at Swindon, as side tanks with 4ft 6in driving wheels, No 1848 being turned out in 1883. It is seen on shunting duty at Taplow in 1907. This locomotive had received saddle tanks in 1898, acquiring panniers in 1919 and a full cab in the 1920s before ending in 1935.

7 *Miscellaneous classes*

Despite the high degree of standardisation introduced by Churchward, there were a number of 'intermediate' and prototype classes that show his influence on designs before Dean's retirement. This was particularly evident in boiler development, which evolved over a period of at least 10 years. This started with the adoption of Belpaire fireboxes, with which locomotives from numerous classes, including the 'Standard' and 'Dean Goods' 0-6-0s and numerous 0-6-0 saddle tanks, as well as the various 0-4-2T and 2-4-0Ts, were rebuilt.

Later Churchward introduced tapered (or 'coned') boilers, which reduced the diameter and weight required at the leading (smokebox) end, where water was at its greatest distance from the heat of the firebox, and concentrated the water over the Belpaire firebox. This also had the advantage that weight was usually concentrated over the driving wheels, at the potential cost of creating excessive axle-loading in this area. 'Top feed', to introduce water from the injectors through clacks beside the safety valves, and the adoption of superheating in many of Churchward's boilers, were further significant developments, but only after the Edwardian period portrayed in this book.

The GWR was also renowned for its rebuilding of classes of locomotives, especially in Dean's era. Sometimes this was an accounting exercise, where locomotives which were effectively almost entirely brand-new were considered, for tax purposes, as merely 'rebuilt'. In other instances most major components were reused, but rebuilding might be associated with the introduction of new boilers, as mentioned above. The GWR was heavily involved in 'converting' locomotives from broad to standard gauge in 1892, most of this being planned well in advance. Some locomotives, from several classes (e.g. '3021' and '3541'), were built as broad-gauge versions of an equivalent standard-gauge class, especially in the late 1870s; these were then readily converted when the time came, and this reconstruction probably required much less planning,

labour and materials than would have been needed for building new equivalents as standard-gauge replacements.

Of all converted classes, the '3501s' and '3541s' were perhaps the most fascinating. Ten of each of these classes were introduced, in 1885 and 1888 respectively, as broad-gauge 0-4-2 side tanks with 5ft driving wheels. They had a reputation for instability at speed, so the '3501s' were rebuilt as 2-4-0 tender engines, and the '3541s' as 0-4-0Ts. From 1892 they were all converted to standard-gauge 2-4-0s or 0-4-4 side tanks respectively. Another interesting case of rebuilding involved the '3511' 0-4-4Ts; from around 1899 the entire class of 40 locomotives, including those never built for broad gauge, were rebuilt as mixedtraffic 4-4-0 tender engines by reversing the cab, boiler and cylinders within the frames!

Churchward also produced, in 1902, a small class ('36xx') of slightly non-standard inside-cylinder 2-4-2 tank engines with 5ft 2in wheels, sometimes known as the 'Birdcage' class, owing to the high-pitched cab. These locomotives were fitted with water scoops for outer-suburban work, but they did not achieve long lives, being in competition with the 'County Tanks' and '31xx' 2-6-2Ts. The purpose of building this slightly non-standard class is not entirely clear to the author, but they seem to have been an enlargement of the basic Dean 'Metro' tank design with a modern Churchward boiler during the period of transition between the two designers.

A one-off locomotive that must be mentioned is Churchward's *magnum opus*, the one and only 4-6-2 Pacific built by the GWR, in 1908, No 111 *The Great Bear*. This engine was effectively a 'Star'-class four-cylinder machine with extended frames and a very large boiler, with wide firebox. Britain's first Pacific, it was not a great success, not least because its weight and wheelbase limited its use to a few main lines, and it worked mainly between London and Bristol. Churchward himself is said to have disliked the locomotive, yet it survived in original form until 1924, when it was rebuilt as a 'Castle' 4-6-0.

'3521' 0-4-4T

The locomotives of the '3521' class underwent some of the most drastic changes of any GWR type. No 3521, built in 1887 as a standard-gauge 0-4-2T, was rebuilt in 1891 as an 0-4-4T. In 1899 it would be rebuilt more comprehensively as a 4-4-0 tender engine by the 'simple' expedient of reversing the boiler, cylinders etc. Perhaps surprisingly, it was to survive in this form until 1931.

Built in 1888 as an 0-4-2T, No 3536 was another locomotive rebuilt as an 0-4-4T in 1891. Destined for further rebuilding, as a 4-4-0, in 1901, it would finally be withdrawn in 1926.

'3521' 4-4-0

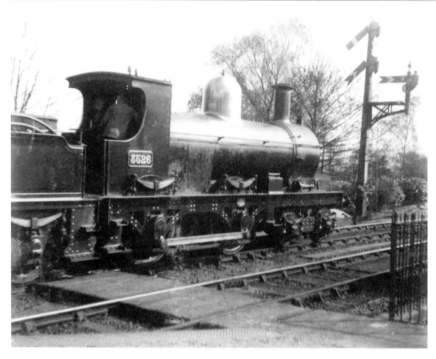

LEFT No 3526 in 4-4-0 form, on the up relief line at Taplow during the winter of 1905/6. Built as a standard-gauge double-framed 0-4-2 side tank in 1887, it was provided with a rear bogie in 1892 and completely rebuilt as a 4-4-0 tender engine in 1900.

BELOW No 3526 again, this time heading a local service (including a van) on the down relief line at Maidenhead in 1907, after receiving this Belpaire-type boiler in the spring. It would eventually be withdrawn in 1927.

ABOVE No 3525, one of the much-rebuilt double-framed '3521s', working in tandem with 'Barnum' 2-4-0 No 3224 on a local passenger service at Oxford in 1906. Note the beautiful turn-out afforded even these relatively lowly machines.

BELOW The last of the first batch of '3521s', No 3540, photographed at Oxford in 1906. This locomotive had been through a similar transition to other members of the class following completion as an 0-4-2T in 1888, involving conversion to an 0-4-4T in 1892 and rebuilding as a 4-4-0 in 1900, when it acquired this Belpaire-type boiler. It would remain in traffic until 1927.

The second batch of '3521s', Nos 3541-60, underwent even greater transformation than the first 20. Built
as broad-gauge 0-4-2 saddle tanks, they later became 0-4-4 side tanks before being re-gauged to standard
and ultimately rebuilt as double-framed 4-4-0 tender engines! No 3557, built in 1889, altered to a 'bogie tank'
in 1891 and re-gauged in 1892, is seen in its final form (as from 1899) on the up relief line at Taplow in 1906.
It would eventually be withdrawn in 1934.

'36xx' 2-4-2T

ABOVE Described as 'four-coupled double-ended tanks' before Whyte notation was adopted, the 31 suburban tank engines of the '36xx' class, featuring a Churchward-type Belpaire boiler and 5ft 2in driving wheels, were introduced towards the end of Dean's reign at Swindon. Here No 3618, completed in 1902, works a local passenger train on the GW main line in 1906.

LEFT In charge of a stopping train, No 3619, built 1902, waits at the down relief platform at Taplow in 1906. Their high-steepled cabs soon earned these locomotives their nickname of 'Birdcages'.

ABOVE Perhaps not the most handsome of GW suburban tank engines, the '36xx' 2-4-2Ts were soon eclipsed by the Prairie tanks of the '31xx' class. Here No 3610 leaves Slough in 1906 with a stopping service on the down relief line. This engine would end its days in 1933.

LEFT No 3617 on the up relief line at Taplow in 1907. Built in 1902, it would be superheated in 1922 and withdrawn in 1933.

Appendices

Table 1: Standard-gauge Singles (2-2-2 and 4-2-2)

Numbers	Class	Wheel arrangement	Driving-wheel diameter	Introduced	Withdrawn	Notes
69-76	69 River	2-2-2	6ft 6in / 6ft 8in	1855/6	1895-7	Rebuilt as 2-4-0s (Table 2)
378-87, 471-80, 577-86	Sir Daniel	2-2-2	7ft	1866-9	1898-1904	Some (23) locomotives rebuilt as 5ft 2in 0-6-0s
55, 999, 1000, 1116-33	Queen	2-2-2	7ft	1873-5	1903-14	Most locomotives rebuilt as 4-2-2s
157-66	157 Cobham	2-2-2	7ft	1878/9	1903-14	Also known as 'Sharpies'
3001-30	3001	2-2-2	7ft 8½in	1891/2	1908-14	Nos 3021-8 built as broad-gauge 'convertibles' and rebuilt as standard-gauge locomotives in 1892; all later rebuilt as 4-2-2s in 1894
3232-51	3232	2-2-2	6ft 8in	1892/3	1918-30	
3031-80	Achilles	4-2-2	7ft 8½in	1894-9	1909-15	New-build version of 3001 class

Table 2: Standard-gauge 2-4-0s

Numbers	Class	Driving-wheel diameter	Introduced	Withdrawn	Notes
149-56	Chancellor	6ft 6in DF	1862	1903-20	First GWR four-coupled express locomotives, built by G. England & Co, heavily rebuilt 1878-83, some with 6ft 8in driving wheels
30, 110-4, 372-7, 1004-11	111	6ft DF	1863-7	1903-14	Built Wolverhampton; used mainly north of Birmingham on secondary services but seen occasionally in the South
20, 439-44	Bicycle (or 439)	6ft 1in	1868-95	1907-18	First Swindon-built 2-4-0s, originally with inside frames and bearings; rebuilt 1885/6
481-90, 587-91*	481	6ft 1in	1869-87	1904-21	Single (inside) frames only
56, 717-26	717 (or 56)	6ft	1885/6	1903-19	Single frames; Swindon replacement for similarly-numbered 1868 locomotives
806-25	806	6ft 6½in	1873	1906-26	Armstrong-built
2201-20	2201	6ft 6½in	1881/2	1904-21	Dean-built
3201-5; 3501-104	Stella	5ft 1in DF	1884/5	1919-33	3501-10 rebuilt from broad-gauge 'convertible' 2-4-0Ts built 1885
3206-25	Barnum	6ft 2in DF	1889	1926-37	Mixed-traffic locomotives
3226-31	3226	6ft 1in DF	1889	1914-22	Similar to '111' class
3232-51	3232	6ft 7in	1892/3	1918-30	Last new 2-4-0s built at Swindon; single frames only
69-76	River	6ft 8in DF	1895-7 (as 2-4-0s)	1907-18	Rebuilt from 2-2-2s

* Other locomotives were added to this class as 'renewals'.

Table 3: Standard-gauge 4-4-0s

Numbers	Class	Driving-wheel diameter	Introduced	Withdrawn	Notes
7, 8, 14, 16	Armstrong	7ft 1in	1894 (as 4-4-0s)	1928-30	Rebuilt from 2-4-0s, built 1886-8; later reconstructed with 6ft 8in wheels as 'Flower' 4-4-0s Nos 4169-72
3252-91, 3312-31	Duke	5ft 8in	1895-9	1937-50	Nos 3312-31 later rebuilt as 'Bulldogs' and renumbered 3300-19 (see below)
3292-3311	Badminton	6ft 8½in	1897-9	1927-31	Class later renumbered 4100-19
3312-72, 3413-32/43-72, 3701-45	Bulldog	5ft 8in	1899-1910	1929-51	Nos 3312-31 rebuilt from 'Dukes'; class later renumbered 3300-3455; of which 29 locomotives rebuilt 1936-9 as 'Dukedogs'
3521-60	3521	5ft 2in	1899-1900 (as 4-4-0s)	1914-34	Rebuilt from 0-4-4Ts, themselves rebuilt from broad-gauge 0-4-2Ts
3373-3412, 4101-20	Atbara	6ft 8½in	1900/1	1927-31	Nos 3400-9 later rebuilt as 'Cities' (see below); survivors later renumbered 4120-68
3400-9/33-42	City	6ft 8½in	1903-9	1927-31	Nos 3400-9 rebuilt from 'Atbaras' in 1907-9; class later renumbered 3700-19
3473-82, 3801-30	County	6ft 8½in	1904-12	1930-3	Nos 3473-82 later renumbered 3800/31-9

NB: All classes were double-framed except the 'County' class, which had inside frames and outside cylinders

Table 4: Dean and Churchward prototypes

Numbers ~	Type #	Driving-wheel diameter	Introduced	Withdrawn	Notes
36	4-6-0; double frame	4ft 6in	1896	1905	Dean (goods) design
33 (2600)	2-6-0; double frame	4ft 7½in	1900	1936	First 'Aberdare'
11 (3600)	2-4-2T	5ft	1900	1933	'Birdcage' tank
100 (2900)	4-6-0 SF	6ft 8½in	1902	1932	First 'Saint'
97 (2800)	2-8-0 SF	4ft 7½in	1903	1958	First '28xx'
98 (2998)	4-6-0 SF	6ft 8½in	1903	1933	'Saint' class
99 (3100)	2-6-2T SF	5ft 8in	1903	1938	'Large Prairie'; renumbered as 5100 in 1929
40 (4000)	4-4-2; four-cylinder	6ft 8½in	1906	1957 (as 4-6-0)	Rebuilt 1909 as 4-6-0 No 4000 and again as a 'Castle' in 1929
111	4-6-2; four-cylinder	6ft 8½in	1908	1953 (as 4-6-0)	Rebuilt 1924 as 'Castle' 4-6-0

~ later numbers in brackets

SF – single (insider) frame; two outside cylinders

Table 5: Early Edwardian goods locomotives

Numbers	Type	Driving-wheel diameter	Introduced	Withdrawn	Notes
79-90, 119-30	0-6-0; double frame	4ft 6in	1857-62	1905-18	
57-68, 316-8	0-6-0; double frame	5ft	1855/6	1908-27	Renewed 1873-90
131-48, 310-19	0-6-0; double frame	5ft	1862-5	1905-25	'131' class
322-41, 350-59	0-6-0; double frame	5ft	1864-6	1912-34	'322' (or 'Beyer') class
21-7/9, 31/2/7-9, 41-4/6/8, 50-53, 116/7, 238/98, 300/70/1/88-412/5/6/9-38/45-54/91-516/93-612/57-716/76-805/74-93, 1012-4/82-115/86-215	0-6-0; double frame	5ft	1866-76	1904-30	'Standard Goods', also known as 'Armstrong Goods' or '388' class
927-46	0-6-0; double frame	4ft 6in	1874	1905-28	'Coal Engines'
2301-60/81-580	0-6-0; inside frame	5ft / 5ft 2in	1883-99	1921-55	'Dean Goods' (one scrapped in 1907)
2361-80	0-6-0; double frame	5ft	1885/6	1928-46	'2361' class
379-81, 384/5/7, 471-77, 480, 577-78, 580-86	0-6-0; double frame	5ft 2in	1900-2	1903-20	Rebuilt from 'Sir Daniel' 2-2-2s
2600-80	2-6-0; double frame	4ft 7½in	1901-6	1934-49	'Aberdare' class
2800-83	2-8-0; two outside cylinders	4ft 7½in	1903-19	1958-65	'28xx' class (inside frames)

Table 6: GWR tender engines in the late-Victorian/Edwardian era

This table demonstrates the decline in the use of 'Singles' and then 2-4-0s and the contemporaneous sharp increase in the use of 4-4-0s and the introduction of 4-6-0s.

Type	1893	1897	1903	1910
2-4-0	197	213	190	147
2-2-2	101	63	30	3
4-2-2	0	65	80	55
4-6-0	0	1	3	77
4-4-2	0	0	0	16
4-4-0	0	45	245	360
2-8-0	0	0	1	31
2-6-0	0	0	80	81
0-6-0	585	693	728	636

(Source: Locomotives of the Great Western Railway, Part 12)

Table 7: Miscellaneous Victorian and Edwardian tank engines

Numbers	Type	Driving-wheel diameter	Introduced	Withdrawn	Notes
1016-75	0-6-0ST; double frame	4ft 7½in	1867-71	1910-35	'1016' class; many later received pannier tanks
202-5/15-22, 517-76, 826-49, 1154-65, 1421-44/65-88	0-4-2T; two inside cylinders	5ft-5ft 2in	1868-85	1905-47	'517' class; Wolverhampton-built; some auto-fitted; some built as saddle tanks and some as side tanks
3-6, 455-70, 613-32, 967-86, 1401-20/45-64, 1491-1500, 3500/61-70/81-99	2-4-0T; two inside cylinders	5ft 2in	1869-99	1898-1949	'Metro Tanks'; Wolverhampton-built; many fitted with condensers – these were generally removed after 1906 and many of the open cabs were closed
727-56, 947-66, 1076-81, 1134-53/66-85, 1228-97, 1561-1660	0-6-0ST; double frame	4ft 7½in	1870-81	1911-46	'1076' ('Buffalo') class; Swindon-built; 50 built as broad gauge and then converted; many later rebuilt as 0-6-0PTs; most cabs were also later closed
93/4, 850-73, 987-98, 1216-27, 1901-2020	0-6-0ST; two inside cylinders	4ft 1½in	1874-95	1906-58	'850' and '1901' classes; Wolverhampton-built lightweight tanks; many later rebuilt as 0-6-0PTs
1813-32/4-53	0-6-0T; two inside cylinders	4ft 7½in	1882-4	1928-49	'1813' class; later rebuilt as 0-6-0STs or 0-6-PTs
3501-20	0-4-2T double frame	5ft 1in	1885	1899 (as 2-4-0s)	'3501' class broad-gauge 'convertibles'; all rebuilt by 1892 as standard-gauge 2-4-0 'Stella' class tender locomotives
3521-60	0-4-2T, 0-4-2-ST or 0-4-4T double frame	5ft	1887-9	1922-34 (as 4-4-0s)	'3521' class, including some 0-4-2STs built as broad-gauge 'convertibles'; all eventually ran as standard-gauge 0-4-4Ts and were later (1899-1902) rebuilt as 4-4-0 tender engines
1661-1700	0-6-0ST; two inside cylinders	5ft	1886/7	1906-34	'1661' class; Swindon-built; most later rebuilt as 0-6-0PTs
905-7, 1701-40/51-70, 1701-1800, 1854-1900	0-6-0T; two inside cylinders	4ft 6in	1890-5	1928-51	'1854' class; Swindon-built; most later rebuilt as 0-6-0PTs
655, 767, 1741-50/71-90, 2701-20	0-6-0ST; two inside cylinders	4ft 6in	1892-7	1928-50	'655' class; Wolverhampton-built; most later fitted with pannier tanks
3571-80	0-4-2T; two inside cylinders	5ft 2in	1895-7	1928-49	'3571' class; developed from '517' class
2021-2160	0-6-0ST; two inside cylinders	4ft 1½in	1897-1905	1907-59	'2021' class; most later rebuilt as 0-6-0PTs
2721-2800	0-6-0ST; two inside cylinders	4ft 7½in	1897-1901	1945-50	'2721' class; many later rebuilt as 0-6-0PTs
3600-30	2-4-2T; two inside cylinders	5ft 2in	1900-03	1930-4	Belpaire-type boilers; 'Birdcage' classic
4400-10	2-6-2T; two outside cylinders	4ft 1½in	1904-6	1949-55	'44xx' class
2221-50	4-4-2T; two outside cylinders	6ft 8½in	1905-12	1931-5	'County Tanks'
3111-49	2-6-2T; two outside cylinders	5ft 8in	1905/6	1937-59	'31xx' class, developed from No 99 of 1903 (see Table 4); later renumbered 5111-49 as part of '5101' class, of which nine rebuilt 1938/9 with 5ft 6in wheels as '81xx' class
4500-74	2-6-2T; two outside cylinders	4ft 7½in	1906-24	1956-64	'45xx' class
3150-90	2-6-2T; two outside cylinders	5ft 8in	1906-8	1938-58	'3150' class, developed from No 99 of 1903 (see Table 4); five rebuilt 1938/9 as new '31xx' class
3901-20	2-6-2T; two inside cylinders	5ft 2in	1907-10	1930-34	Rebuilt 'Dean Goods' (2491-2510)